CONTENTS

Introduction: How Coddling Kids Is Killing Kids Confidence

"What will I learn from a boxing coach about parenting?"

Many parents are concerned about how they are parenting their child(ren) nowadays. A lot of modern-day parents are worried about their kid's safety, lack of confidence, and mental health challenges. With all this uncertainty, boxing has become an outsourced solution for helping parents with a variety of their concerns. As a boxing gym owner, I have been on the frontlines of seeing these shifts for a couple of decades now. Since I started my boxing gym on April 30, 2011, I have encountered many situations when parents would come to me with their parenting challenges, seeking help with their children's dilemmas. To address these concerns, I've used my boxing gym to create a safe space for people to feel comfortable being themselves. That environment has allowed me to ask the "tough questions" to kids that typically their parents are too afraid to ask (or don't want to hear). Those conversations helped me learn the REAL truths of what people are struggling with and understand how to help solve their challenges.

What parents can learn from the mindset of a boxing coach is not just about how to inspire discipline, but also about understanding their child's needs and challenges better. This understanding can help parents connect with their child(ren) on a deeper level while also fostering a sense of reassurance and empathy. What parents need to learn to enhance their relationships with their kids, is that they need to renew their credibility with their child(ren) every day. Youth are rebels by nature, so they like to go against the grain or be protected by familiar sources (e.g., mom, dad, grandparents, etc.). They want to explore their options and will respond differently to whatever authority they're under. That means kids will test you every day to figure out how they feel a parent (or authority figure) will hold them accountable.

Every day, parents need to show up as their best selves and be the best representation to earn their child's (ren's) respect. As a parent (or anybody working with kids), you must be a person of accountability. Kids want to know that you will do what you say you're going to do and will quickly lose respect and credibility for those who don't stay true to their word. For parents to be the type of role model that influences youth to listen like a boxing coach, they must embody the standards, values, and lifestyle that they want their child(ren) to mimic.

Over the years, I have helped thousands of students overcome immense challenges. Parents have come to me to help their children stop suicide attempts, self-harm, and increase their self-esteem. But what I've learned is that taking a kid to the boxing gym only deals with the symptoms of their problems and doesn't solve the deeper issues that brought them to that state of mind. Instead of waiting for more kids to show up to my boxing gym already "broken," I want to be proactive to stop these behaviors before they even start.

Writing this book is my attempt to solve some of the root causes of negative mental health outcomes in younger generations, and addressing my concerns to modern-day parents and others responsible for helping raise younger generations. I want parents to realize how they may be contributing to some of their children's behaviors (and what they can do about it). I want parents to develop the "voice of a boxing coach" at home through establishing standards, improving their communication skills, and adopting a positive leadership approach like I use in the boxing gym. If taken seriously, parents should become better role models themselves while also seeing positive adaptations in their child's (ren's) mindset.

Off the back, I want to let you know that I am NOT a parent. Some people will try to immediately discredit me and say that I'm "not qualified" for trying to give parenting advice. However, my experience teaching academically and athletically for over two decades has given me A LOT of experience with working with kids (and their parents). It might be true that I am not a parent, but my credibility comes from having EVERY job where parents outsource their kid's activities outside their home. I have been a teacher, tutor, "at-risk" mentor, counselor, coach, after-school provider, gym owner, AND more. My experience working with kids (and their parents), nonprofit organizations, and school systems has allowed me to serve as a resource (and liaison) to help solve problems involving youth throughout America. I want to offer parents advice on how to influence their children and allow millions of families to reap the positive results I achieve in the boxing gym every day.

"What is the mindset that parents can learn from a boxing coach that can be applied to raising their child(ren)?" Why should parents want to learn to "parent" like a boxing coach?

A great boxing coach is like a sensei, therapist, surrogate

parent, and best friend all in one. The level of responsibilities and multitasking roles a boxing coach administers can rival any Fortune 500 CEO. On any given day, a boxing coach must cater to people's changing moods, different personalities, work ethic, and varying attention spans. On top of that, you must be motivational and encouraging to work with. Parents can learn how to use these different skills to become better leaders for their children (and themselves).

From most likely practicing boxing themselves as kids, boxing coaches have the confidence to live their truest selves "out loud" (and parents can learn a lot from that). Living "out loud" means being your most authentic self with maturity and not compromising on your non-negotiable principles. Non-negotiable principles mean not compromising on your beliefs or lowering your self-respect for the approval of others. It also means living up to a standard that you will be proud of within yourself and not feeling guilty for standing up for what you believe in. Because courage breeds influence, that toughness is transferable and can be contagious. When parents have a high self-awareness about themselves (and their actions), that creates a mature environment with high standards for others around them to live up to. Younger generations need examples of noble leaders to learn what's possible and provide structure and reassurance for their well-being.

One of the most important tips parents can learn from a boxing coach is to live a lifestyle of character and maturity. Boxing coaches are just like parents because both are goal-oriented and want the best results for those they lead. However, what boxing coaches do best is make the most uncomfortable situations feel comfortable (which breeds confidence and a high degree of self-worth). That mindset is needed in the "real world," and boxing coaches are constantly focused on preparing youth for the realities they will face in the future. What parents can learn from a boxing coach is how to master the psychology of the mind.

Being astute for combat is not just for fighting inside the ropes but also for learning to overcome challenges outside it as well.

Why is coddling so bad for children?

Every parent I know wants (what they think is) the best for their child(ren). They all want to be the best provider they can be and feel like their children's happiness is placed mainly upon what they can do to provide for them. Modern-day parents find it hard to find the balance between giving their child(ren) the best upbringing possible and helping them be driven to do for themselves. When kids grow up and are used to getting what they want only by asking their parents (and they constantly provide for them), they lack appreciation for the work it would take them to own what they have. If that same child had to work themselves to take the risk to earn that gift, they would appreciate that luxury (or necessity) totally differently. I believe coddling is bad for children because they lack learning lessons that could improve their character, it also decreases and worsen their mental health.

When parents coddle their kids, it slows down their developmental process of learning how to deal with stress effectively and reduces the chances of building resilience. When a child wants something (or is challenged), a parent should assess the situation to see how they are modeling to their child how to respond to it. Every mistake, misunderstanding, or praise a parent makes can be interpreted by their child(ren) about how they should handle situations later in their own lives. Parents should instill more discipline in their approach to giving their child(ren) what they want by considering the longevity of their responses and protocols to administer lessons they want their child(ren) to learn from.

Coddling is usually done when a parent sees their child having a hard time and wants to rush in to help solve any worry their child may have. For instance, if a child is frustrated about something they are struggling to figure out, they will express some level of dissatisfaction (e.g., complain, cry, etc.). Instead of parents wanting to solve their child's discontent right away, parents should wait until they see how much effort their child puts into solving their own challenges before volunteering to help. Then, parents should wait until their child asks them for help before they attempt to talk them through what they are challenged with. That's an important point because if parents do the task for their child right away, their child won't truly learn how to solve the intricate details for themselves later if faced with the same problem.

As a parent, the next time that you see your child start to struggle with learning something new, follow these steps:

(1) Take a deep breath.
(2) Slow down your temptation to react.
(3) Wait for them to ask you first.
(4) Seek to assist (without doing for the child).
(5) Ask them questions about what they've done to solve their challenge (especially for older children).
(6) Work with them through a counseling approach to have a dialogue to help them solve their issue independently (so that the child can learn how to mature from what they're going through).

Our job as adults is not to take the pain away that our kids may be experiencing but to help them make sense of the pain so that they can learn to overcome their trials or tribulations.

When parents remove new struggles that their child(ren) can learn from, their child(ren) loses opportunities to develop self-accountability and become better independent thinkers. When children are coddled, they grow up lacking confidence and self-efficacy. If parents could practice creating a bit of mental distance before reacting to their children's discomforts, they (and their children) could become more disciplined in how they handle situations. Coddling is a mindset that is disruptive to a child's growth and can negatively impact their mental health and well-being as adults in the future.

Why should parents share this book with other parents?

Every parent wants to learn how to be a better parent and looks for trusted resources to give recommendations to help them along the way. Parents need help raising their child(ren) because having a kid is not meant to be a one-person job. Learning skills and tips that work to get kids to want to be more mature can enhance a parent's effectiveness in leading their child(ren). All parents should want their child(ren) to become the next greatest dentists, teachers, doctors, and politicians with ethics that we can trust. When parents share this information to help other parents raise their child(ren) better, it can empower those families and generations to come from what they can learn. There are multiple benefits that a parent can be rewarded with by sharing this book with other parents. These include things like engaging in book clubs and discussing what they will apply to their parenting skills together, having conversations with other parents about how to improve their own behaviors toward being better leaders for their kids, and so much more. All good parents want other good parents to thrive in parenting together.

Part of being a good parent is sharing resources (like this book) to enhance the lives of other parents, families, friends, and the greater community at large.

We as adults must do more nowadays to help not just the child(ren) we are responsible for but also their friends, their friend's parents, and others in the ecosystems that we influence. This book is meant to share proven actions that have improved the mindset of thousands of younger generations through academic and boxing training environments. I want parents to inspire their child(ren) to become their best selves through their example. Even if you think that you know the most "perfect" parent or a single mom working multiple jobs to keep a roof over her family's head, ALL parents are struggling to get the hardest job in the world right (parenting).

On behalf of myself and the greater society, I would like to say, "Thank you!" for being willing to share this resource for the advancement of future generations. When parents do a great job, society thrives. The information you are willing to share with other parents will have a lifelong impact on their children's lives, other families with influence, and even those you will never know you impacted. "Thank YOU!"

How did I get started working with kids (and parents)?

I started working professionally with kids (and communicating with parents) after teaching as a 5th and 6th-grade elementary school teacher. But before then, I had a job working at a gym called "3rd Power Fitness" in Washington, D.C. It was at 3rd Power Fitness that I learned how to box, and I went from being a student taking boxing classes to being employed working multiple jobs at the gym. I did EVERY job that was available at the gym. I worked at the front desk, taught boxing classes, and did 1-on-1 personal training. As much as I loved working at 3rd Power Fitness for the years I was there, I was on my way to graduating college and put the word out there that I was looking to find more consistent work (like a salary job).

Trying to find a job after college was frustrating! For months, I went door to door and looked online to find something I could do (and be paid well for), but many jobs required years of experience and expensive certifications. So, I asked anybody at the time to let me know if they could help me find employment and kept applying online while I worked at 3rd Power Fitness.

One day, I got a hit back from my mechanic (I told you I talked to EVERYBODY), and he told me about a job opportunity to become a part-time physical education (PE) teacher at an elementary school. When I contacted the employer at the school (a guy named Mr. Abubakar Senghor), he gave me an interview to meet with him and the principal (Dr. Ron Taylor). When I arrived at Emery Elementary, I was greeted by Mr. Abubakar Senghor (the Dean of Students at the time) and Dr. Ron Taylor with warm greetings. The interview went so well that within the first interview, not only did they want to hire me, but little did I know that they needed multiple jobs filled and that I fit the profile they wanted for multiple positions.

As the interview progressed, Dr. Taylor had an amazing intuition about me. He saw something that gave him pause and wanted to take a chance on me. Midway through the interview, he had a vision of thought that I could be best utilized in an academic classroom. He was shifting jobs around that year to fit what culture he wanted at the school, and he saw me as an independent male thinker who could make a substantial improvement to help lead his all-boys 6th-grade class (the school was gender segregated at the time).

While we were discussing my background during a round of questioning, Dr. Taylor paused the interview, didn't say a word (for what seemed like the longest minute in history), and asked me if I ever thought of being a teacher in a classroom. I told him that I always knew I could teach because earlier in grade school, when my friends wouldn't understand what was being discussed, they knew they could come to me to find out how to break down what was being taught in classes. If I knew what the teacher was saying, I could help translate information for them to learn in a way they could understand. After hearing that answer, Dr. Taylor asked me if I would be interested in teaching a 6th-grade all-boys class full-time (instead of getting the part-time "PE" position). I ABSOLUTELY jumped at the chance and decided to take the 6th-grade teaching job. Because of my mechanic, who referred me to Mr. Senghor, which led to Dr. Taylor's decision to take a chance on me, my life has been forever changed...

I taught for two and a half years at Emery Elementary School and learned A LOT about parenting and the education system. I learned that kids bring their home standards and behavior to school with them, and whatever kids are going through at home, they bring that same attitude with them to school every day. For example, a student at Emery Elementary School was always getting in trouble at the beginning of the day, and the principal's office would always send him to me to have me talk to him for a few minutes to calm him down. He was always fighting and getting in trouble because he would be late to school (and he hated people feeling like he wasn't responsible).

That student came from a background where 22 people lived in the same house (with three generations and three last names). Besides knowing that student, I also taught his siblings, cousins, and uncle in my classes, and they all shared the same bed every night (3 to a bed). All of the same kids had to share the same bathroom before school every morning, and the young man that I would talk to would be angry most times because he was one of the youngest in the house. Almost every morning, everyone would make him late because he would have to shower and eat last all the time. I understood how that could make a person upset, and he needed to be reassured that he was okay and wouldn't be left out at school like he felt at home.

Reputation matters, and Dr. Ron Taylor saw I could help with these types of realities that students from inner-city neighborhoods were going through. I saw a lot of myself in my students and knew the demands that needed to be met and solutions to solve their challenges. I came from the same inner-city background they came from, so I could literally be a roadmap to helping them see my perspective. Since I was an older version of them, what I had to say could relate and help make sense for them to understand situations. Not only did I help countless students like the young man I calmed down many mornings, but in my first year teaching academically, I also helped start an aftercare program at the school (tutored grades 1-6 for 3 hours Monday through Friday), coached the boys basketball team, and became 2nd in charge of the chess club.

In going into my second year of teaching, Dr. Ron Taylor called me in to meet with him before the school year started. When the meeting started, he began asking me how my summer had been and then explained how he thought I exceeded his expectations the previous year. During the meeting, he "braced" me for an ask because he was making more teacher changes again (I believe he had a budget shortage). With confidence, he decided to up the ante again, but this time, he asked me if I would be willing to teach TWO grades at the same time! I must admit that this request threw me off a bit. I was puzzled, not because I was scared, but because I had never been a student in a two-grade classroom system before (let alone know how to teach two grades simultaneously). Once he explained how the 5th and 6th grades were very similar in lesson training and that I would have some students go to special education classes (for most of the day), I believed in his confidence in me and didn't hesitate to take on the challenge.

That 2nd year, I did more than expected of me in the first year. Not only did I teach 24 boys (total) academically, but I also became the head of the chess club, still taught the aftercare program every weekday, coached the boys AND the girls' basketball team (and took the girls to the DC City championship my first year coaching them). I will ALWAYS show much love and respect for what Dr. Ron Taylor did for me, and I owe him a GREAT debt of gratitude for taking a chance on me. Those first experiences teaching at Emery Elementary gave me vital experience in learning how to adapt to leadership positions. Not only that, but I learned how parents "parent" their children (and the outcomes it produced). Those beginning teaching years at Emery gave me invaluable experiences that I still learn from to this day. I will always keep building on an opportunity given to me years ago and pay it forward by improving whoever I will interact with for years to come.

Conclusion to introduction

I wrote this book for parents to discuss, debate, and analyze how they can reevaluate their parenting behaviors. So far, it has been an honor to help assist thousands of parents with raising their child(ren) through my academic impact and extra-curricular activities with youth. Since becoming a boxing coach, my focus has ALWAYS been to help people feel better about themselves by learning something from me that could improve their mindset. The mindset that I want parents to get from thinking like a boxing coach is one of self-accountability, developing a growth mindset, and being honest with children about future adulthood responsibilities. The hope is that by helping parents work on themselves, they, in turn, will be able to lead their child(ren) by their example. I hope everyone who reads this book walks away feeling more mature through an increase sense of self-awareness and knowledgeable about leading themselves, their child(ren), and contributing to the greater community at large.

The first chapter covers a parenting behavior I call "Butler Parenting." "Butler Parenting" is a form of parenting behavior where parents always look to insert themselves as "saviors" whenever their child faces any initial hardship or discomfort. It's the kind of behavior you see when parents do a task for their child when their child could easily do it for themselves. It is a coddling practice that parents think is a harmless and generous act, but it creates a mindset in their kids that whenever something gets too frustrating, their parent (or guardian) should step in and "save" them from their distress. This act of "Butler Parenting," in my opinion, is crippling the critical opportunities for kids to develop emotional maturity and slows down their developmental problem-solving skills.

The second chapter discusses how parents must learn to lead themselves better so that they can more effectively lead their kids. I believe that it is almost impossible to know how to lead others unless you learn how to lead yourself first. When parents learn to develop their own self-awareness practices, they can use what they learned to be better-proven leaders for their kids.

In Chapter 2, I talk about "The 7 Basic Self-Mastery Focuses" that parents can use to become the best version of themselves. The "7 Basic Self-Mastery Focuses" are framed in an acronym called "RAADD GF" (a.k.a. can be remembered by the saying

"Rad Girlfriend"). "RAADD GF" stands for R-Routine / A-Action / A-Adaptation / D-Decisions / D-Discipline / G-Goals / and F-Faith. I created this concept to help people think about ways they can improve their lives through a mindset shift. Each focus has its own importance in improving a parent's mindset (or anyone's life). "RAADD GF" (a.k.a. "Rad Girlfriend") emphasizes the benefits of adopting these applications to increase a person's efficiencies and life outcomes.

I will also introduce another concept I call "The 5 Wellness Practices." This chapter mentions these focuses to help parents consider important priorities that impact their wellness directly (and indirectly).

The 5 Wellness Practices are:

Financial
Physical
Material
Community
Relationships

Each has a priority in adulthood that must be addressed to create a well-balanced lifestyle. The focus on each category is to help parents see the importance of improving each aspect of their overall lifestyle.

I also created another acronym in Chapter 2 called "D.I.E.T." I bring awareness that your "diet" is more than just what you eat (it's also everything else that your mind and body intake). The time you invest in things like what you watch on TV, the type of music you listen to, the people you hang around, and other things you "ingest" all impact your mindset.

The breakdown of what "D.I.E.T." means is:

D - Dietary Behaviors
I - Information Intake
E - Entertainment Pursuits
T – Thought Training

I break down each topic to help parents see how what they spend time on can improve their mindset or create barriers that slow their personal progress.

The **third** and last chapter discusses how parents can better prepare their child(ren) for the realities of adulthood. So many kids lack the understanding of what they should be preparing for as adults, and they are totally unprepared for "adulting" when they are of age to be an adult (typically 18 years old). I address my concerns by helping parents with a structure of topics I think parents should help their child(ren) learn about adulthood called "The 3 Adulting Awarenesses." These awarenesses are Finances, Health, and Life Skills. Along with these topics, I have subtopics that specifically detail awareness to help parents talk to their child(ren) about what to expect as adults when they get older (e.g., bills, aging, networking, etc.). I argue that parents should expose their kids to "adulting" realities as early as possible (e.g., taxes, wellness practices, communicating, financial responsibilities, etc.) because these are awarenesses they will inevitably face. As youth get older, they will have a MUCH harder time adapting and understanding how to cope with "adulting" if they aren't being educated about what to expect. More than ever, preparation for adulthood is needed to help youth learn how to make good decisions because the pace of the world is moving faster, and youth are more susceptible to needing to adjust to unforeseen challenges quickly.

I also address a mindset that I think parents should help their child(ren) develop called "Learning how to L.E.A.R.N." This focuses on helping younger generations learn essential skills that are necessary to become successful adults. "Learning how to L.E.A.R.N." breaks down into an acronym for people to remember, which is: L – Listen / E – Emphasize / A – Articulate / R – Retain / N – Negotiate. I elaborate on each topic as to why I think younger generations should practice getting better at each focus (and how parents can help).

For some parents, this book is NOT for them. If you feel like your child listens to everything you say and does everything you ask them to do (and you don't have any behavioral questions about your child), then maybe you have a "special" child and have it all figured out. But for most other parents who are looking to learn more about leading their child(ren) better, there is something in this book you can learn from.

This book is for "grown folks" who want to have the "tough conversations" about parenting and aren't afraid to be vulnerable about their parenting needs and curiosities. There is a real need to speak openly about parenting, and I want this book to be a resource to help parents improve their confidence, their parenting influence, and the mental health of their children.

Let's make this book "controversial"! I say "controversial" because when people start talking about their kids, they become excited from their heightened emotions (and word spreads faster)! But this energy should be directed towards making parents hold themselves to a higher standard (and encouraging other parents to do the same). It will help parents raise future generations that will contribute to improving the greater society (which is what we ALL want).

As a parent, your child(ren) will closely watch how you lead yourself and decide if they will take your advice on what results they see in you. When you get YOU right, your relationships, personal wellness, and everything else improve because of your decisions. To make that happen, parents must do personal work to be the best version of themselves and to help the next generations learn how to work better independently (and with others). By learning the stoic wisdom of a boxing coach's mindset, parents can learn solutions to "Butler Parenting" challenges, improve self-awareness, and improve their children's chances of success when living independently as adults. I hope you enjoy your reading and look forward to learning ways to become a better parent, person, and positive influence in the environments you are a part of.

CHAPTER 1: BUTLER PARENTING

When people hear the phrase "Butler Parenting," their ears perk up. They want to know what it means but are also curious to see if their parenting style fits the description. Butler Parenting isn't a slight or a compliment, but a consistent behavior in which parents take over tasks their children should be learning how to do on their own. Parents take a personal stake in ensuring that their child doesn't feel inadequate or frustrated for doing something "wrong." Instead, parents insist on doing the task for their child to ensure a desired result. Instead of letting their child(ren) be challenged in moments where they can test their potential, parents fear their child(ren) will be embarrassed by failure and want them to avoid that feeling as much as possible. Many modern-day parents practice taking over a task or responsibility that could cause stress in their child's life at the moment. In turn, they feel like they are being a "good" parent for doing the task so that their child does not struggle or get upset when handling it on their own. It's a temporary dopamine hit for parents, but in the long run, it slowly deteriorates their child's abilities to learn patience, grit, and deal with uncertainty.

As a boxing coach, I have trained children as young as four years old and adults up to 81 years old at my boxing gym. Everyday for at least the past 13 years (and more if counting my academic teaching career), I have been in positions to learn about the needs of children directly (and indirectly) and have been concerned about the mental health and wellness of younger generations for years. I've impacted thousands of lives by offering boxing classes, 1-on-1 personal training sessions, coaching amateur and professional boxers, and even trained professional MMA fighters at my boxing gym. A lot of parents bring their child(ren) to get trained by me because they believe that boxing will increase their child's confidence, help them lose weight, and even help with mental and physical disabilities.

Since I started Donte's Boxing Gym in 2011, I've coached youth with boxing training to help them overcome some of their life's challenges. It's been a gratifying experience, but training sessions in the boxing gym only go so far. I have seen too many times that my students will change their behavior and attitude while being with me, and as soon as the child(ren) goes home, they fall back into the same habits and lose their motivation to keep up their discipline (the same happens with adults). The progress made in the boxing gym often lasts while the person is in the gym, then the temptation of eating snacks in the comforts of home lacks the consequences from an enforced standard. To make lasting change, children need consistency from their parents to reinforce high standards, discipline, positive attitude, and continued mindset improvement like they are expected to make in the boxing gym.

Over the past few years, I have been getting growing concerns from many parents wanting to get their child(ren) into boxing for various reasons. Some parents want their child(ren) to become more disciplined or cross-train for different sports, but the most popular reason parents want their child to box is to help their child gain more confidence. However, the most sought-after reason kids want to learn how to box is to work off stress. Boxing is the ONLY sport that people want to extract all the benefits from athletic training but do not ACTUALLY want to do it. For instance, I've had situations where parents would want their child to get into boxing to improve their "footwork" but not want them to get in the ring actually to practice boxing. But the reason why boxers have such great footwork is to avoid getting hit! Imagine being inside a boxing ring where a person's whole objective is to damage you with legal blows. If you're smart, you will get your feet moving as quickly as possible to avoid the onslaught of punishment (that's why boxers move so quickly)!

Over the years, I've learned that when parents typically want their child(ren) to box because their child has low confidence, they have already sensed (or are worried) that something is "off" with their child. The parent has seen some evidence of the need to do something to help their child, and it has gotten to a point where they can no longer feel like it's a passing emotion. They are either concerned about their child's mental health and low social self-esteem or even want to outsource consequences to get their child to be more disciplined. But here's the thing. Boxing only helps soothe the symptoms of the problems (not the underlying cause). What needs to happen is a more profound action to solve the root cause of WHY the child is being recommended to come to the boxing gym. Boxing shouldn't be used as a solution to solve problems but as a therapy to work off the stress while overcoming the issues being worked through.

The first time I ever received an inquiry about boxing training for youth, was from a dad wanting to get help for his daughter who was committing self-harm (aka cutting herself). In a panic, her dad had come to me not knowing what to do, and in a last-ditch effort, he came to the boxing gym because he heard I was good with people (and decided to seek my help). As I spoke with the concerned dad, I listened to all the efforts he had tried before he came to me. After listening to what he had to say, I felt that I should meet his daughter to learn from her and ask why she felt so stressed to the point that she was committing self-harm. I told the dad that if we had a good initial conversation, I would offer her the chance to work with me, and if she liked that option, she could take it one session at a time. He went back home and talked to her about it, and she agreed to talk to me to find out if she would be interested in learning how to do boxing training.

When she finally came to the gym, I was surprised. She was tall, pretty, intelligent, and had a chill demeanor. As I started talking with the young lady, I found her to be very kind and humble. She answered questions with deep thought and a willingness to engage. I asked questions to figure out who she was and what she was interested in initially. Afterward, I turned the conversation to why she thought her dad thought it was a good idea for her to learn how to box from me. She felt she understood why her dad was concerned and thought she might want to box to let out stress. She expressed that she was under a lot of pressure from her parents to do well in school, and her way of "relieving" her stress was through "cutting."

As the high school-aged young lady was explaining her reasons for cutting herself, she admitted that she did so because her parents were overbearing, and she felt that it was hard trying to find her own identity. As her dad stood quietly next to his daughter, listening to her point of view, it became apparent to him that he needed to lower his standards so that their daughter wouldn't feel so pressured to live up to his high expectations. I kindly explained to the young lady that her parents were trying to do for her what they felt was best from what they knew how. I talked to her about my perspective of how I didn't realize how much parents sacrificed to give so much to their kids until I got older. I shared that when I started to pay my own bills, I had a WHOLE new respect for my parents after realizing how expensive it was to afford things after living on my own. After I shared some more words of wisdom, I asked the young lady to hug her dad to show him how much she appreciated him bringing her to the boxing gym, and they both smiled and held each other tight for a nice moment. As we were finishing up our discussion, I asked the young lady if she would be interested in learning how to box to relieve any more stress she wanted to let out, and she smiled and said, "Yes."

The moral of sharing that story was to show that the root cause of the young lady's problems was that she felt overwhelmed by her parent's high expectations. The pressure she felt was like a pang of deep guilt that she couldn't make her own mistakes out of fear of disappointing her parents. She had learned to internalize her frustrations and not feel like she could share her REAL feelings with her parents (out of fear that she would disappoint their feelings). That led to her being frustrated and not knowing how to handle negative emotions. So, she decided to do what her friends did when they were stressed (self-harm by way of cutting). For a few months after our initial conversation, I worked 1-on-1 with the young lady and she LOVED the progress she was feeling within herself. I'm glad to report that after she started working with me, she had stopped cutting herself and is living successfully, making herself (and her parents) proud.

In recent years, I have witnessed many parents who have high expectations for their child(ren) and are constantly worried about their safety. They feel like they must be involved in EVERY aspect of their child's life, and if they're not, they don't feel like they are being a "responsible" parent for their child(ren). Another concern modern-day parents have is that they don't want to let their child(ren) out of their sight and are constantly catastrophizing that something terrible is going to happen to their child if they aren't around to "save" them all the time. The unlikely worst-case scenarios and wanting to "failure-proof" every situation their child could experience, is not only not bad for parents, but it's also bad for their child(ren) too.

With good intentions, parents try to do everything they can to give their child(ren) many opportunities and make their lives as "easy" as possible. However, parents must mature to realize that learning to overcome failure is a part of life. Learning how to fail is a lesson in building grit, determination, and developing maturity. When parents are constantly interfering when their children are attempting something new, parents are inadvertently weakening their children's ability to develop resilience without realizing it. In response to their worry, children are developing mental health challenges that result in depression and many forms of anxiety.

Every day, I witness so many children (including young adults over 18) whose parents feel like they need to try to control every aspect of their child's (ren's) outcomes. Many parents mess up their children's lives by not allowing them to learn how to make decisions and take accountability for their outcomes (good or bad). When children don't learn how to make decisions and handle stress, they will not build the emotional maturity to handle "adulting" when they become adults themselves. As children grow up and learn what strengths (and struggles) they can work on to improve themselves, they will need to independently face struggles and challenges to develop a sense of self-efficacy.

Modern-day parents have taken the position that they want to be their child's(ren's) "best friend" and don't ever want to see their child(ren) struggle or be frustrated. Instead, parents are doing EVERYTHING possible to remove stressors from their children to provide a childhood of endless fun and lack of stress. Modern-day parents are coddling their children so much that younger generations are experiencing a livelihood of prolonged adolescence well into their adulthood. Ironically, the lack of disappointment that parents are trying to get their child(ren) to avoid, is causing them to develop mental health challenges, from depression to many forms of anxiety. Many modern-day children don't know what to do when faced with responsibilities on their own and rely on their parents for a lot of their basic needs (even as adults). For instance, I know of parents who call their college children every morning to wake them up and still do their laundry for them because they don't know how to do it themselves. Some parents I know don't want their grown children (over 18 years old) to drive by themselves and will even fly across the country to take them to meetings to be there in case they need them.

My concerns about how modern-day parents are raising their children come from a place of wanting to see younger generations do well for themselves as adults. However, what I've experienced from working with children (and their parents) has led me to want to address many of the underlying problems I see daily. When I see parents always doing the simplest things for their child that their child should be doing on their own (e.g., tying the shoes of their 18-year-old son, etc.), it gives me pause.

I see firsthand how many young people are struggling with depression and anxiety, and I believe that a lot of the root causes are how children are being coddled by their parents. Instead of seeing these problems and not doing anything about them, I want to address my concerns through dialogue with modern-day parents and be a catalyst for change. It starts with addressing modern-day parents' behaviors and the ways in which they are raising their children.

Witnessing many parents wait on their children "hand and foot," I've seen how their children adapt to getting what they want based on the standards of the expectations from their parents. A child will see what a parent will respond to with an inquiry (e.g., "Mom/Dad, I can't do this?") just to see how their parent will respond. They will internalize the level of reaction from the parent and use that as a comparison for a later ask. Children are constantly gauging the authority they're under to see what it will take to get what they want. Children are perfectly fine with their parents taking their struggles away, while not having to labor to get what they want. However, when children grow up believing that whenever they face adversity, their parents will always "save" them, they will lack the coping skills to handle adversity on their own as adults themselves.

I believe that there is an unconscious parental practice that is hindering modern-day youth's developmental maturity. It happens whenever parents start to see their children feeling stressed and then act to impose their will to "rescue" their children from their discomfort. When parents interfere and jump into action to take over whatever is making their child slightly stressed, they are unconsciously conditioning their child to quit and let someone else deal with their "pain" or discomfort. That mindset doesn't change easily. Unfortunately, children learn and repeat those awarenesses growing up (even in adulthood) and continue to expect those same reactions from other people outside of their homes (e.g., teachers, coaches, bosses, etc.). When children grow up expecting others to "rescue" them, they can easily resort to complaining and making excuses (even blaming others) for outcomes that don't go their way. When parents respond to this outwardly stressful behavior their child displays, their anxiety-induced response to "save" their child is what I call "Butler Parenting."

What is "Butler Parenting"?

Butler Parenting is when parents interfere with their child's ability to learn how to work through stress (by doing their child's tasks themselves). It is a coddling behavior that parents display in the moments when they witness their child frustrated, and they immediately act to take over what's uncomfortable for them. In moments when a parent decides to do Butler Parenting behavior, they feel almost overwhelmed (or even have feelings of "guilt") when seeing their child struggle slightly over the smallest of tasks. The problem with Butler Parenting behavior is that it disrupts opportunities to help a child learn how to deal with adversity. When a child doesn't learn how to deal with stress, it also slows down their ability to develop emotional maturity (from not learning how to become patient and disciplined). The effects of Butler Parenting lessen a child's abilities to problem-solve, develop confidence, and cause mental health challenges (e.g., depression, anxiety, etc.).

When parents witness their child experiencing complications, they must choose to view those uncomfortable situations as preparation for the "real world." Children need to learn how to deal with the realities of negative emotions (and failures) as they grow up. Having experiences of learning how to encounter failures allows a person to learn how to figure out problem-solving strategies. When opportunities for children are removed from facing discomfort, they lack the ability to think independently, have low problem-solving abilities, and don't develop the patience to learn new skills.

I have seen SO many times parents do EVERYTHING they can to appease their children and still feel almost "guilty" if their child has any need for anything. Modern-day youth have been coddled by their parents so much that they believe that their parents will always do for them what they don't want to do themselves. Having responsibilities like domestic work (e.g., cooking, washing dishes, laundry, etc.) are not skills that modern younger generations have been accustomed to learning, and some feel like they will never necessarily need to. For example, I had an 18-year-old (let's call him Larry) who's never had a job and whose parents cared for his every need. Larry was one of my 1-on-1 personal training clients who came to see me weekly to help build his confidence and self-esteem. Larry's dad would accompany him to every personal training session to keep an "eagle's eye" over his son and watch over him to ensure he could care for his every need. One day, after I greeted the father-son duo, I immediately recognized that Larry seemed a bit sleepy. In a lighthearted and joking way, I asked Larry, "What time did you go to bed last night?" with a shy grin, he answered, "Probably around 2..." With a quick joking jester, I yelled out, "2 am :)?! Didn't you know you were coming to train with me today??" And he chuckled and shook his head up and down as to say, "Yes."

I felt like I might need to learn more about how well Larry was feeling, so I asked him, "What time did you get up this morning?" He then answered, "Right before I came here." (it was almost noon). I then turned our conversation towards talking to him about being more prepared for adulthood, giving him some "real-life" talk to get him to think about his future (before he's out on his own and grown). I told him that he needs to learn how to cook (along with some other things) and not have to wait for someone else to feed him when he gets older. With a look of disbelief, he just smiled and shook his head. I said seriously but jokingly, "You do know that your mom is not going to cook every meal for you for the rest of your life, right?" With a cocky grin and look of surprise, he smiled while shaking his head as to say, "I don't believe you..." I instantly turned to his dad and told him, "You better tell him that his mom isn't going to be cooking every meal for him when he is an adult and out of the house!" He said with a look of shy agreement, "I don't know Donté, she just might!" Smh.

Modern-day children have it "too easy" and aren't getting a "reality check" before they face the hardships of the "real world."

When parents practice Butler Parenting, it delays children's ability to learn how to take accountability for their responsibilities. If youth grow up never having the experiences of learning how to overcome adversity (or doing things they don't want to do), when they become adults, it will be harder for them to learn how to accomplish problem-solving. Before children grow up and have adult responsibilities, they need to practice learning how to handle rejection, deal with stress, and not quit when experiencing failures. As adults, we are already familiar with the fact that all of these realities are essential to becoming successful in adulthood. My suggestion for parents is to allow their children to struggle to face adversity and give them the opportunity to learn from it. When children gain more experience facing hardship, they become better when challenged and have the maturity to know how to get things done independently.

Parents must learn that letting their children experience uncomfortable situations is necessary to help them learn how to handle things on their own. By allowing children to struggle to handle challenges creatively, they can practice taking small risks and performing problem-solving skills that can help them later in life. This is a prerequisite of "adulting." To help younger generations learn from their adversities, adults (parents) must help children learn how to develop emotional maturity from encountering stressful situations independently.

WHY should parents STOP "Butler Parenting"?

Parents should stop Butler Parenting because it deteriorates a child's willingness to learn how to work through stress. One of the actions I see parents do way too often is as soon as their child starts to whine or complain at the beginning of a task, they jump right in and take over the tasks from their child. Instead of immediately stopping the child and taking over their learning "opportunity," parents should help their child assess what they're doing right and what they could improve on. If the child continues to complain, the parent can offer to help by talking through what their child should do while having them still take the lead. A hands-on approach can be a good option when initially showing a child how to start something, especially when you know you will have them practice what you've shown them immediately after you're done. Then, allow them to try the entire pursuit on their own for their own experience (this ensures that they learned what you've showed them).

Children need their parents to prepare them through mentorship when experiencing stressful situations and model maturity through a lens of assurance. Parents should also help youth by asking them questions about their concerns, helping them think about why they feel frustrated, and helping them learn how to be calm while figuring out their challenges. It's not that they don't need their parents to never come to their aid, but it is wise for parents to understand that their child needs to learn how to develop the skills of grit. Beyond getting a good education, skills like having grit, knowing how to communicate with others, and being able to experience rejection are essential in preparing a child for adulthood. When parents come and take over things their child should be learning to grasp on their own, it doesn't help youth learn how to develop patience, mature from their mistakes, or practice discipline to work hard to finish the task they started.

There are three main reasons that I believe parents should stop Butler Parenting:

(1) Butler Parenting stalls a child's problem-solving abilities.
(2) It creates an expectation for kids that when something feels too difficult for them to practice (or try), they should expect someone to come and save them (or quit trying).
(3) It makes a child more lazy and less confident.

Below are explanations of why these three reasons make sense for parents to stop Butler Parenting:

Butler Parenting stalls a child's problem-solving abilities.

Part of the learning process for understanding most things requires a bit of a willingness to suffer. Not so much suffering to the point of a "survival of the fittest" situation, but suffering in a way that makes you concentrate on learning how to do something new. Learning new things can be frustrating because you have to be vulnerable and take a risk to find out what happens next. Confronting those realities will create a level of high character that demonstrates the patience, maturity, and discernment needed in adulthood.

The value of letting a child learn to get comfortable getting uncomfortable is immense. That requires parents to be open to allowing their children to discover new information that can challenge their beliefs and practice being patient within themselves to stretch their imagination. Learning new things can initially be irritating and make a person feel defensive because it's challenging to admit when you're not aware or good at something. When a parent disrupts the process of their child learning from being irritated, the forging process of developing grit gets lost because the child is not learning how to process struggle.

Childhood is meant to be a "practice ground" for learning how to respond to challenges, develop maturity, and handle the hardships and uncertainty they will face in adulthood. Butler Parenting delays confronting discomfort when parents interfere while their child is experiencing something new. Children are supposed to learn from frustration, and parents should use those moments to build up "mental callousness" in their children to help them learn how to problem-solve.

It creates an expectation for kids that when something feels too difficult for them to practice (or try), they should expect someone to come and save them (or quit trying).

In the boxing gym, I've had plenty of situations when a parent will see their child having to experience a bit of hardship and try to comfort the child immediately. Then, if the child says that they don't want to finish the session, allow the child to quit and walk away. The mindset that children develop in their minds from those experiences is that when anything gets too hard for them (or they feel any discomfort), they should stop what they're doing and look for an excuse to quit. That way of thinking will not be helpful for youth as they get older and become adults. A lot of "adulting" is doing hard things that a person doesn't want to do, and having the mindset to get tough things done.

Learning how to develop maturity involves experiencing many hardships. Children should learn how to govern themselves when they're irritable and frustrated into learning how to turn their annoyances into creating solutions. One of the marks of good parenting is allowing their child(ren) to work on turning their impatience into progressive thinking. There will be plenty of times as children grow up (and become adults) when they will feel frustrated and want to quit. When children get upset about not doing something right (or not figuring out something as fast as they would like), parents should help their child(ren) frame their frustration as a "gift." Learning how to change their mindset from wanting to get rid of hardship and turning it into a lesson will make them solution-makers. This is an important skill to help younger generations figure out how to mature and learn from adversity.

Gaining those earlier experiences helps youth later in life better handle their work responsibilities, increase personal relationship skills, and develop emotional maturity. Children need to learn how to figure out their frustrations independently from their parents through their own life experiences. It is a skill that will be helpful to them in adulthood and needs to be cultivated in childhood as early as possible. The opportunities for children to experience struggle should always be considered a privilege and not a problem. Parents should help introduce more learning challenges into their children's lives to help them think more (not less). Children are much more resilient than their parents give them credit for. If you're a parent, the next time you see your child start to get frustrated while working on a task, allow them to "sit" with their frustration for a while. This will allow them to develop patience and learn how to mature to figure out their own challenge. The "opportunity" to face adversity is for a child to learn from what they're going through, and if they ask for help, to offer advice first before working to help them. It's also important to make sure not to take over the task for a child at the first signs of them being frustrated. Instead, allow them to learn from why they feel frustrated and help ensure they learn how to finish what they started. Reframing their struggle as a good "opportunity" will help children to get smarter in ways that will help them become better problem-solvers for their future.

It makes a child more lazy and less confident.

When parents raise a child(ren), they set a standard of what leadership a child(ren) should expect from other authority figures they interact with. When kids interact with other authorities outside of their home, they expect to be treated with the same (or better) acceptance and tolerance their parents give them at home. What permissions parents make acceptable at home with their child(ren), sets expectations and standards of what their child(ren) believes should be granted in the greater society. When parents practice "Butler Parenting" behavior, they're unconsciously showing their child(ren) that this is how authority is supposed to respond to them when they're stressed. Children start to interpret that whenever their stressed, someone else should always show up and take their frustration over for them. That can lead to a mindset of making excuses when things don't go their way and blaming others when expectations are unmet.

What Butler Parenting takes away from children is the practice of getting something wrong (even multiple times) and developing the courage to try again. Almost everyone will fail at something the first time they try it. But when a person develops a mindset to outdo the first attempt, that mental process creates much maturity for those who don't quit. When parents practice Butler Parenting behavior, they inadvertently make their child(ren) lazy and less confident. For children to develop lasting self-esteem and grit, they must be taught to take their "pain" and turn it into progress. By reframing their stress perspective, children should learn from their parents to focus on creating positive outcomes (even while experiencing discomfort).

Children should be taught to develop a mindset of being more curious when facing challenges and learn to turn their frustrations into excitement. That mindset shift can help children creatively come up with solutions to solve their problems independently of their parent's assistance. Children should be taught to be invigorated when challenged and focus on positive thinking to help them reframe their frustration into solutions. These reasons are some examples of why parents should stop "Butler Parenting" behaviors to help their child(ren) become more resilient later in life.

Why should parents help their children learn "real world" responsibilities earlier in life?

Over the years, I have created jobs for ex-juvenile offenders by partnering with the Maryland Department of Juvenile Services, and created opportunities for students to earn their Student Service Hours (SSL Hours) to be able to graduate from high school. I did this to assist youth with the opportunity to develop more "real world" experiences and show them the "behind the scenes" work of what it REALLY takes to run a business. I've offered three different positions at my boxing gym (front desk, assistant instructor, and greeter) and taught each student every position so that they could learn more responsibilities. The reason behind offering these opportunities for youth to work at the boxing gym is that I always wanted to know what it would take to REALLY become successful (but didn't know how). So, when I created my own business, I wanted to use my business as a platform to help youth learn what I wish I had known when I was younger.

Overall, the experiences of the youth who worked at the boxing gym were very educational. The students got the chance to get "real world" experience by interacting with the public that visited the gym and learning how to take on leadership responsibilities working with their peers. Here's a testimony of one of my students (Will) who earned his student service hours (SSL hrs.) by working with me at my gym:

"Working at the gym means a lot and has a whole meaning to it when working here because when your working in the gym you can learn a lot more than the average boxer, you can learn a lot of techniques, combinations, how different people are judged by their skills and why there are different groups in the gym: level 1, the level where kids are still improving and their in the beginner level, level 2 where kids are at a stage where they have a little experience and know a little with what their doing but still need some help, and finally level 3 where they shouldn't and don't need any help whether it's sparring, Putting gear on or even just how they act when their in breaks because when your on breaks groups 1 and 2 tend to talk a lot but with group 3 they give each other their own pointers to themselves saying to themselves how they should improve on their own. Working in this gym gives a whole reason why I should be here because me being here can get me real experience in the real world knowing how to handle a job because if I have a job you would have to know everything that goes around it and how to handle everything if there's not an adult around, I should and do know how to handle things if a random person comes into the gym and asks a random question about the gym weather if it's if "the gym has an open workout?" I will say all the things to assure the person how to handle Dontes Boxing because I know how much this means to me so I have to know how to handle being with this job and the first step to doing that is to work out with people in the gym who don't know how things go around at Dontes Gym. The other thing is this gym is more than boxing its not just fitness and training it's about the learning experience and getting out of your comfort zone to feel comfortable when doing something that used to be uncomfortable to you."

It is important for youth to be exposed to experiences that will further enrich their lives. By providing my former worker (Will) with the opportunity to learn "real world" responsibilities, he learned a lot of life lessons about himself and the people he worked with at the boxing gym. It was a "Win-win" for both of us. I felt satisfied that I had given him the exposure I wished I had when I was his age, and Will learned new skills from his experiences working at the boxing gym. For the rest of his life, Will is going to apply what he learned from his experiences at the boxing gym and add more value to his family, friends, and the greater community.

What are some examples of "Butler Parenting"?

The actions of Butler Parenting are what parents look to do for their kids when they are fully capable of doing what they are asked (or required) to do themselves.

Below is a list of examples to give the best description of what "Butler Parent" behavior looks like:

- When parents are constantly panicking over every little mistake their child makes and tries to "save" their kid from any stressful situation.
- When a parent feels like their child can't handle something they are doing on their own, and out of frustration, they choose to take the lead in doing what their child should be learning how to do independently (even when not needed or asked).
- Doing or taking over responsibilities that an adolescent, teenager, or young adult can do on their own (e.g., opening a water bottle, putting on their shoes, speaking up for themselves, etc.).
- Obsessively seeking their child's validation and asking

what they can do for their child ALL THE TIME!

- Parents who fear being "unavailable" for anything their child wants and look to "drop everything" they're doing just because their child wants them (no matter how frivolous and small the ask is).
- They always want to keep a "watchful eye" on their child(ren) at all times (even under supervision) and NEVER want them out of sight in fear that they will want them for ANY reason.
- Willingly acting as their child's personal "Uber driver," taking them anywhere they want to go at a moment's notice.
- Obsessively checking on their kids through texting, calling, or tracing their whereabouts (on their cell phone), even if they know where their child is.
- Checking websites and apps like Zangle obsessively to see their child's schedule and grades at school multiple times a day!
- They want to take care of all their child's (ren's) needs (and wants) and never want their child(ren) to feel like they can't live without them.

These behaviors (and more) are just examples of things that describe Butler Parenting.

What should parents do when their child struggles with a new challenge?

To help youth learn how to overcome stress, they need to encounter challenges to gain experiences while growing up to learn how to face adversity. Parents must realize that when they remove obstacles from their kids, they remove opportunities for their own children's potential. Going through struggle is a way to learn new things about yourself and prepare for future hardships. When parents see their children struggling to figure out something, they shouldn't begin to panic. Instead, parents should allow their child(ren) to face adversity and reframe it as an opportunity for their child(ren) to learn how to solve problems creatively.

Everyone alive will face challenges, and the way we deal with those challenges teaches us about our strengths and weaknesses. After experiencing what we are capable of, we can make better decisions about how to improve ourselves (and discover who we are). Being curious about what can be learned through exploration and taking risks will give you experiences that will shape your character and integrity.

Those valuable moments when a child sighs or complains about not knowing how to complete a task are a GOOD thing! Those moments are opportunities for parents to help show their kids how to learn to work through adversity and not quit until they solve their own frustrations. In the introduction, I mentioned a tip to help parents think about their response before attending to their child when they see them frustrated. I want to reintroduce those six steps parents should take when they see their child(ren) struggling with a new challenge:

(1) Take a deep breath.
(2) Slow down your temptation to react.
(3) Wait for them to ask you for help first, then offer your assistance.
(4) Seek to assist (resist taking over what the child is struggling with yourself). Let the child learn from their experiences.
(5) Ask them questions about what they've done to solve their challenge.
(6) Work with them through a counseling-like approach to help them independently solve their issue. Children need to learn how to work through solving their own problems to help them mature into adulthood.

Parent's behaviors show their child(ren) how to
respond to situations based on their reactions.

When kids make mistakes, the first thing they do is look around to see the reaction of those around them (and then see how they should respond). If children see their parents "freak out" when they make a mistake, then they will match that energy and panic themselves. Parents set the precedence to the appropriate level of response in their children's reactions and behaviors. For instance, when something breaks, spills, or a child is in pain, the level of urgency their parent (or other authority figure) administers makes that child react with the same level of concern or panic. Or if a parent yells at their child every time they make a mistake, their child will internalize that making mistakes makes people upset with them. That can lead to a child becoming mentally hardened (and sensitive) and not want to try new things. A child will internalize how to respond to situations based on their parent's rewards (or reprimands) and justify their behaviors based on what they've experienced from their parents.

How parents deal with situations with their children will affect them for the rest of their lives. Children often repeat what their parents do (and say) and use it as a barometer of what is "standard" in the "real world". As parents, it all starts with how you lead yourselves and what behaviors you are modeling that displays to your child(ren) how to respond when facing adversity. Decisions and behaviors that parents make when their child(ren) is challenged in difficult moments can impact how their child(ren) responds to future situations. Parents must use their influence to the best of their ability by modeling a great example of standards that prepare their child(ren) for the "real world."

T.I.P.S. (Takeaways / Insights / Perspectives / Stories)

T.I.P.S. is to help the reader remember at least three things before moving on to the next chapter. Throughout this chapter, I have made points about how parent's behaviors impact their kid's lives. Below, I wanted to reinforce points that I made earlier in the chapter to help parents not forget a few points within the chapter. Some reminders of thought are:

- What is Butler Parenting?
- There are three main reasons that I believe parents should stop Butler Parenting.
- What are three examples of Butler Parenting?
- What are the six steps to follow for parents to stop themselves before administering Butler Parenting behavior?
- Parent's behaviors show their child(ren) how to respond to situations based on their reactions.

(1) What is "Butler Parenting"?

Butler Parenting occurs when parents are uncomfortable witnessing their child being frustrated and respond by quickly attempting to take over their child's perceived discomfort.

(2) There are three main reasons that I believe parents should stop Butler Parenting:

- Butler Parenting stalls a child's problem-solving abilities.
- It creates an expectation for kids that when something

feels too difficult for them to practice (or try), they should expect someone to come and save them (or quit trying).

. Makes a child more lazy and less confident.

(3) What are three examples of Butler Parenting?

. Obsessively seeking their child's validation and asking what they can do for their child ALL THE TIME!

. Obsessively checking on their kids through texting, calling, or tracing their whereabouts (on their cell phone), even if they know where their child is.

. Doing things for their kids (or taking over responsibilities) that a child can do on their own (e.g., opening a water bottle, putting on their shoes, speaking up for them, etc.).

(4) What are the six steps to follow for parents to stop themselves before administering Butler Parenting behavior:

(1) Take a deep breath.
(2) Slow down your temptation to react.
(3) Wait for them to ask you first (before you come to help them learn to solve their dilemma).
(4) Seek to assist (without doing for the child).
(5) Ask them questions about what they've done to solve their challenge.
(6) Work with them through a counseling-like approach to have them solve their issue independently (without a parent's assistance) so that the child can learn how to work through solving their own problems (as a lesson to mature).

(5) Parent's behaviors show their child(ren) how to respond to situations based on their reactions.

CHAPTER 2: THE JOB OF PARENTING STARTS WITH SELF-MASTERY

To become better parents, parents must first seek to master themselves to be a better example for their child(ren). By confronting areas in their own lives that they can improve on, parents can teach their child(ren) how to build their confidence from their own example. Since parents are the initial role models their kids look up to, it's important that parents become the best version of themselves to influence their child(ren) in positive ways.

I believe there are 7 Self-Mastery Focuses that can holistically help parents become the best versions of themselves (or anyone). When people improve themselves through self-mastery practices, they can then offer advice to help others do the same. By learning how to master these 7 Self-Mastery Focuses, individuals can develop personal skills to help them become more confident, mature, and have better emotional intelligence. To help remember the 7 Self-Mastery Focuses, I created an acronym along with a phrase that can best help people remember them called "R.A.A.D.D.G.F." (which can be remembered as a "Rad Girlfriend"). It's a corny phrase, but it's a way to help people recall a particular focus when wanting to practice self-improvement.

The 7 Self-Mastery practices are:

R-Routine

A-Action
A-Adaptation
D-Decisions
D-Discipline
G-Goals
F-Faith

The 7 Basic Self-Mastery Focuses

R-Routine

Developing good routines is a skill for enhancing a person's confidence and self-worth. Routines can also help a person become more reliable and consistent with decision-making. I feel so strongly about the importance of having good routines that I think it should be a mandatory subject taught in grade school every year. Developing daily efficient routines is important because people will get good at anything they practice long enough. The rote practice of doing the same thing over and over makes getting desired outcomes easier over time (as well as lessening anxieties). It is a skill that should be discussed and learned to take more seriously because people who are good with routines are usually great bosses, coworkers, and friends (because they are reliable).

The key to starting a good routine is knowing WHY a person wants to make changes in the first place. Deciding to start (and continue) a new routine is hard. A person must eliminate as much doubt and excuses to quit as possible because they will have valid excuses that will make them want to quit (before they even start). Creating merits to measure outcomes can keep a person motivated to continue progress until they've achieved their goals. While tracking progress, a person must try to keep the same level of intensity that got them started in the beginning. It can help to put reminders everywhere as "nudges" to help a person with their decision-making throughout the day. Things like handwritten notes in hard-to-miss places, alarms on a person's phone, and other cues can be greatly effective in keeping a person focused on achieving their goals.

On the other hand, when people don't practice developing good routines, they are usually more likely to be unreliable, lazier, and lack positive outcomes. Thus, it causes difficulty working, socializing, and prioritizing appointments with people who aren't great at prioritizing their time. The way that a person treats their time can dictate everything else in their lives. A sense of self-awareness to prioritize scheduling tasks will enable a person to have more self-respect towards their time and respect for other's time as well.

The US military culture is a great example of a structure that helps people with establishing good routines. It doesn't matter what background a person comes from, the US military can transform the majority of people who join any of the six branches into "routine machines." Even long after a person has left military service, they still follow the habits they learned from their time in the armed forces (just ask anyone who's served). I believe that more structures in today's society (e.g., schools, businesses, etc.) could benefit from taking a page out of the military culture and taking what system they use to help civilians become better at establishing good routines.

Trying to create a new routine requires more energy to meet new demands (and adjust to more work). Some new routines could include working out to lose weight, eating healthier, or making schedule adjustments to prioritize some kind of new endeavor (e.g., salsa dancing, etc.). Routines are behavior changes that a person decides to do to improve themselves in some way.

It is never easy to change a routine (and be consistent about it), but it does get easier over time when consistently practiced.

There will come a time when the urgency that made a person start a routine will become bland and unexciting. However, a person must find ways to get reinvigorated, not become complacent, and continue to work to accomplish their goals. A person must work harder once they get used to making initial progress and plateau. To further progress, a person must make smaller goals to keep themselves motivated until they achieve what they set out to do. Results will come from compounding consistency and a person seeing measured progress paying off later from their efforts.

A-Action

Taking action is a significant step in applying a person's will because it turns goals into reality. When a person decides to act, they are moving with the intention of accomplishing an outcome they desire. There is nothing like the challenge of taking action. From the expectations that are trying to be met, to the memories being formed, action is needed to make anything possible.

A person must become a risk-taker to overcome the uncertainty of moving towards the unknown. Being able to move when you are afraid or act when you have doubts is a practice. You must want to see a result irritatingly enough not to experience that feeling of dread from regret. To avoid that feeling of not knowing what an outcome could have been if a person had tried, a person has to PRACTICE taking ACTION! People must take strides in moving towards the outcomes they want to discover, from working backward from what it will take to get there. To help a person make progress toward what they want to accomplish, some easy options are to make a "To-Do-List," write things down on a calendar, or do whatever to help nudge themselves to achieve their goals.

When a person takes those initial steps, they create momentum, which is a powerful force that is hard to stop when it takes shape. Anyone can propel themselves to create momentum. It takes having a goal and acting on their curiosity to take the first move. Showing the courage and willingness to be vulnerable, having a positive attitude, showing discipline, and focusing on achieving an outcome are all ways to enhance momentum. To conclude this section, taking action is a commitment. It expresses what a person is willing to do to achieve a thought.

A-Adaptation

Another big part of self-mastery is learning how to adapt. When pursuing any goal, a person will inevitably need to adapt to the demands of their circumstances. Being adaptable makes a person better at creating relationships (e.g., romantic partnerships, work-related, etc.), being appropriate in multiple settings, or making others feel comfortable in the same space. It is a skill that can help a person feel more confident and feel like they belong in multiple environments. Adapting well could mean being able to speak up to create alliances or being stealthy not to draw any attention to oneself.

Learning how to adapt is important because life is constantly evolving, and dealing with uncertainty is a constant reality. No matter who we are or where we are at any given point, we are constantly learning to adapt to our surroundings. With every conversation we have, in every environment we step into, or any time we travel, we, as humans, are constantly adapting to everything around us.

As a boxing coach, I must adapt to people's attitudes, personalities, and moods on a daily basis. From session to session (or class to class), I deal with people who are depressed, anxious, less confident, and have a lot on their minds. The number one tip I would give to anyone looking to become better at adapting is to stay curious about what's happening around you (e.g., people, events, etc.). Adapting a mindset to be flexible is key to being a leader and can be applied to every aspect of a person's life.

I believe that the main advantage of learning how to adapt is being mentally able to be comfortable in any situation. Being good at adapting helps you interact better with others in different environments and makes you an asset under any circumstance. Whether showing up at a dinner party, asking a person out on a date, or getting a new job, learning to adapt to any situation is a skill that is essential for adjusting to many conditions.

D-Decisions

Decisions are important because they give a person direction toward their desired results. Decision-making is like voting to become the type of person you want to become (or the outcome you want to attain). Before making decisions, a person should be clear about what goals they want to achieve while choosing to make uncomfortable trade-offs to accomplish them.

To practice decisions toward self-mastery, a person should have a clear concept of what they want to experience and know why they want to accomplish their goal. The decision-making process involves questioning the emotional trade-off of a desired outcome and planning to make the goals achievable. A person must also figure out the pros and cons before making a decision and make an informed judgment to convince themselves to charge after their desired outcome (or not).

There are numerous results from decisions made, but there are three kinds of decisions that lead to outcomes: good, bad, and indecisive. Good decisions are assessed by whether a person gets whatever they set out to do. It is assumed that if a person makes a good decision, it will result from their ability to be "smart" and think rationally. However, we should not give so much weight to believing that all good decisions come from people being "geniuses." In fact, we should acknowledge that "good luck" or "being blessed" are factors that contribute to outcomes as well. Bad decisions are seen as undesirable results that don't go as planned, and a person can be blamed for not thinking "smart" and being naive. The outcome of bad decisions can be seen as either unintentional or by mistake. It could result from a lack of information, bad timing, or egotistical thinking. It is through frequent practice of taking risks and self-reflection that a person can get better at decision-making over time. Lastly, indecisive decision making usually comes from not feeling completely informed and not knowing what to do at a certain time. Having moments of indecision require more information, reflection, and overcoming feelings of potential failure.

Regardless of which decision a person's makes, it requires making the best judgment call with the best readily available information (and hope not to regret your decision). Every decision should be based on being a better person for your future (and others) and creating positive results that contribute to the greater society at large. To succeed in making good decisions, one should think long-term about the outcomes they want achieve and what happens after they get what they want. Ultimately, being a better decision-maker will make a person more confident in their ability to make a sound judgment. This is a focus that should be prioritized and practiced often.

D-Discipline

Being disciplined helps a person align their mindset with their actions to execute whatever they want to accomplish. Most people rarely "feel" like practicing discipline because it's hard work to overcome their mental discomfort. Practicing discipline is rarely "fun" because it usually involves physical labor in less-than-satisfactory circumstances. The rote practices of performing discipline are boring and exhausting, but getting good at discipline improves developing patience and learning how to do new things.

When a person practices being disciplined, they are working on the outcomes that they can control. Whether it's working on self-improvement, a domestic task, or a work assignment, being able to prioritize getting things done takes focused effort. To master discipline, you must be OBSESSED with accomplishing the hard things you set out to do. You must figure out how to FORCE yourself to focus on that goal so deeply, that in your mind, you don't want to know what life would feel like if you didn't accomplish it well. Instead of looking at discipline as a labor you don't want to do, reframe it as a process that helps you do (and get) everything you want. The great benefits of developing discipline are helping with improved focus, higher intelligence, reliability, and many other positive traits.

G-Goals

Setting goals is an important way to create a positive mindset. When people look forward to accomplishing something new, they can muster up incredible amounts of energy from being motivated. Other reasons why people set goals are wanting to learn a new skill, overcoming a setback, or deciding to change other priorities in their lives. Creating goals is "the point" of why you want to do (or attain) something. When a person knows why they want something, it creates passion within them to take the risk of going after what they want. To achieve goals, a person should create as many reasons as possible to make them personally important to themselves. I believe that anyone who wants to achieve anything in life MUST become as singularly focused on it as possible (to finish what they started). Being obsessed with a desired result lessens opportunities for distraction, gives direction, and fuels ambition.

To accomplish goals, a person must be patient and realize that it may take longer (and sometimes cost more) than expected. Sometimes, people underestimate the difficulty of what they want (or want to become) because they have never done it before (and are a bit naive). A good mindset to adopt when pursuing goals is to have a positive mindset while being optimistic. When pursuing goals, a person will feel vulnerable and not as confident from being inexperienced. When trials and tribulations happen, a person must shift their mindset from dread to hyper-focusing on what outcome they want to feel after achieving what they set out to do. Whether a person wants to lose weight, graduate, or set their sights on achieving a numerical goal (like saving money), they must strive to be extremely intentional about what they want to accomplish. Making plans and setting markers to see smaller progress (e.g., creating a "To-Do-List," charts, etc.) can help a person accomplish goals a bit easier. There is nothing like that "feeling" after accomplishing a goal and the acknowledgment that you learned in the process from the work you put in. Goals are like food for our brain, and we need to feed off them to keep us going...

F-Faith

Having faith allows trust to be possible, confidence to be created, and belief in abiding by agreements to be made. Without faith, a person would never take risks or try something new. I believe faith is critical in basically everything that we do. Without having faith, a person would never get started on anything that they want to achieve. To produce faith, a person must visually look forward to seeing an outcome and then work to achieve it. That "feeling" of confidence to act on proving something is possible (without any evidence that it will come true yet) is called "Faith."

The practice of faith turns belief into real-life realities. I believe that having faith is essential to having confidence and is a prerequisite for all success. It works not just for the big or small unknowns but for everything in between. None of us knows what the future holds, but our personal convictions give us reassurances that things will work out in our favor.

There are plenty of examples of faith being executed in our everyday lives that we often don't appreciate. Before we get on an airplane to take a flight, we have faith that it will take off and land safely to help us get to our destination. We demonstrate faith when people start their cars and believe that it will cut on without any problems. Even before we eat or drink anything, we have faith that it won't give us food poisoning or negatively affect our bodies. There are SO many examples of risky situations where outcomes aren't guaranteed, but we still do them because we have faith that everything will work out just fine.

Little Faith vs. Big Faith

I tend to title faith in two categories: "Little Faith" and "Big Faith." A person typically uses "Little Faith" when they do something that they are used to doing a lot and take for granted (like when things are "normal" for them). For example, a person may have faith that they will arrive at their routine destination safely or believe that they will see an old friend or family member again without something bad happening to them. "Little Faith" is when there is little to no regard for risk, and plans are made fully believing that they will "automatically" come true.

But then, a person can experience what I call "Big Faith." Sometimes, supernatural situations result in people desiring "Big Faith." Situations like a person trying to beat a cancer diagnosis or "free solo" climbers who climb steep mountains without much protective equipment, are examples of people projecting "Big Faith." Developing "Big Faith" stretches one's consciousness (and rational mind) and forces a person to think bigger than what they know is possible.

Developing faith is an expression of expectation. It is a mindset that shows a person's confidence in their belief and their willingness to overcome whatever challenges they face to get what they want. Believing in faith is a deep self-awareness practice that isn't something on the surface that other people can see. It is a belief that whenever a person feels they can put their mind to accomplish something, they truly believe they can achieve it.

Some benefits of practicing having faith are:

* Being able to handle stress better from having less anxiety.
* Being self-assured that everything will work out for your greater good.
* Having confidence that what you plan to overcome will happen.

Prioritizing Overcoming Procrastination

When parents (or anybody) would like to improve themselves, they should first know why they want to change. A person should be clear about the objectives they want to enhance about themselves and create substitutions to replace old ways of doing things. When people see things within themselves that they want to improve on, it can feel discouraging or even a feeling of discomfort from "not feeling good enough." Those insecurities are tough to deal with, and a lot of people don't like to view themselves in a negative light. However, when a person wants to change themselves, it takes a willingness to be vulnerable and a desire to address weaknesses in their character. For a person to face their fears, doubts, anger, and insecurities, they must make them priorities that they want to deal with. If not, they will become harder to deal with in the long run, and the longer a person puts them off, the less likely they will overcome those deficiencies (if they ever have the courage to face them).

Most people try to wait until they "feel like" dealing with their problems, but waiting makes things harder and more complicated. In my experience, I've learned that the longer you put off doing something you don't want to do, the more expensive, inconvenient, and time-consuming it becomes. A solution to solve challenges is to schedule a time to address the nagging issues ASAP (e.g., "To-Do-List," mark a time on a calendar, create time to seek help, etc.). By prioritizing scheduling and addressing undesirable issues, a person is more likely to overcome those challenges simply by making efforts not to "run" from them anymore. When people start to see progress from prioritizing and addressing their challenges, their anxieties lower, and they feel more confident about accomplishing the goals they initially procrastinated about.

The best way to become a better parent is to first improve on becoming the best version of yourself.

When you, as a parent, understand how to develop a mindset that can positively transform yourself, you become an agent of change for others to learn from (especially your children). By how you live your life as a parent (or other authority figure), you become a source of knowledge that can influence your kids in so many ways. Kids want to look up to their parents (and others) and be inspired by accomplishments that show their value. To become the best parent you can be, you must prioritize better self-wellness practices (e.g., positive attitude, working out, financial success, etc.) to create the version of yourself that you would like replicated in those around you (especially your children).

The 5 Wellness Practices

Becoming a better parent starts with being a good person. Parents should at all times be making the best decisions toward being a positive role model for their kids. To be able to lead others, you must first be able to lead yourself well before others will trust your advice. A modern-day parent doesn't have the luxury of telling their kids, "Do what I say, not what I do," and expecting their kids to look up to them with reverence. Parents must take accountability for areas of their lives that they can control, and that includes looking at five key areas to improve their overall well-being. I created a list that I believe could help parents (or anyone else) improve their personal wellness called "5 Wellness Practices."

These five categories include:

* Financial
* Physical
* Material
* Community
* Relationships

Financial

Financial goals are essential to a parent's wellness because they help secure resources, provide opportunities for personal advancement, and build confidence (for themselves and their kids). Being financially responsible helps parents achieve a standard of living where they can afford assets and liabilities toward their family's lifestyle. Whether it's saving up for an expensive purchase (e.g., a home, car, etc.), investing, or saving for emergencies in the future, how a parent earns money and manages their financial life is important.

Most adults were NEVER taught financial literacy in school. Even while growing up in our households, conversations about money were never central to our upbringing. There was never any urgent need to think about (let alone talk about) taking care of ourselves as middle-aged or elder-aged adults. As teenagers and young adults, we were more focused on earning money for frivolous things like fashion (to impress people to date) than on saving to invest in our futures. It wasn't until people started to graduate college (or start to live independently) that money became a central focus for survival.

From learning from our experiences, I believe that much more education should be taught to youth to prepare them for financial realities BEFORE they become adults. Starting in elementary school, youth should be taught the basic principles of budgeting, investing in stocks, opening a bank account, and other financial information. The goal of raising youth is to become successful adults who can take great care of themselves, and part of that involves learning financial literacy.

When people aren't educated on money, they tend to have a "spend first" mentality because they are teased with so many advertisements all around society. That "YOLO" (aka You Only Live Once) mentality leads to a more frivolous lifestyle. That can be very detrimental to a person's future options (as opposed to a save first to live longer mentality). Lacking financial literacy is actually a liability not just to individuals but to the greater international community at large. People who tend to grow up without financial literacy typically have bad spending habits, end up owing a lot of debt, and have a harder time trying to afford goods and services (from always struggling to pay back bills and loans). On the other hand, when people learn financial literacy, they learn to think long-term about how to use money more strategically for their future. Instead of getting money to spend on liabilities, a person will think about saving to invest, buying assets that become tax advantages (like property), and starting businesses.

If parents want to be better at improving their financial literacy, they can research excellent sources of information on YouTube, TikTok or listen to podcasts (e.g., Earn Your Leisure, etc.). On a broader scale, governments should do much more to create more opportunities to help their citizens become financially literate. They can do so by funding school curriculums and after-school financial education programs to help their citizens become sufficiently financially literate. The investment through government-funded assistance programs would recycle back to the government from a better-educated society. That investment would contribute to more citizens attaining higher-paying jobs, which in turn would have citizens pay higher taxes. The amount of taxes paid on everything from income tax, sales tax, and property tax would offset any initial investment and circulate money in the economy, I would think, by at least 10x.

Since a subject like "Money" isn't taught in schools (and isn't really discussed by parents either), most people tend to have to learn about financial literacy through "trial and era" as they get older. Because of the lack of basic academic training in financial literacy, a person must learn what financial information can help them accomplish their personal goals independently. Unfortunately, there isn't a "one-stop shop" where a person can learn everything about financial literacy (besides the internet), and even then, there is a lot of mixed information. As a result, people are left to figure out on their own how to manage whatever money they are responsible for. Some are swayed to "gamble" to hire a financial advisor that they find out about through word-of-mouth or "cold calling" a local bank (which is very risky to hand over all of a person's money to someone they don't know). There should be a better path toward financial literacy besides searching the internet or getting lucky by hiring a "random" financial advisor. Parents and governments should be more proactive in educating themselves (and their citizens) about financial literacy and not wait until adulthood to "figure it out." This aspect of wellness deserves more urgency because the need for higher financial literacy benefits not only families today but also future generations of society as a whole.

Physical

Parents should consider taking care of their bodies a mandatory priority for becoming better parents. It's not just about the physical benefits but also the psychological advantages. By prioritizing their health, parents can lower stress, develop more focus, and be more present for their child(ren). This is a critical step towards ensuring longevity as a parent and enjoying parenthood for as long as possible.

Besides exercising, many parents are still very unaware of how food impacts their minds and bodies (as well as their children). Most people may know that exercising and eating healthier is good for them, but they're incentivized by convenience (and price) and LOVE the taste of sugary, salty, and fatty foods. Instead of parents waiting until they experience physical health scares that frighten them into action, parents should proactively address potential threats BEFORE they become problems they have to deal with. Taking preventative measures like eating highly nutritious meals and exercising often, can help parents live a life of less physical pain and health concerns. It may cost parents more upfront, but it will be less expensive over time when they don't have high medical bills and medications to purchase to stay alive.

Unfortunately, we live in a reactionary culture in America where we are used to responding to concerns until after they've become too painful to bear. I have made a career of helping people with physical health concerns, and see the realities of all kinds of health concerns on a daily basis. I usually see people interested in working out after a doctor tells them that they have something wrong (or is getting worse) with their health. Then, people react by being motivated to work out to quickly lose weight to reverse their problem (or trying the latest fad diet). As much information is available to educate people about how to take care of their health, it is STILL hard for people to change their ways. However, it's not ALL their fault. The general public is influenced by the constant marketing of businesses selling unhealthy popular foods (e.g., fast food, chips, sodas, etc.), which are more affordable and more convenient to purchase. With the teasing of seeing fast food through commercials, and government agencies that allow food companies to add ingredients that cause cancer (and other health concerns), no wonder people are having a hard time learning how to become healthy (it's more difficult).

When parents take care of their physical wellness, they can positively affect their children's health as well. Over the course of my boxing coaching career, I've had thousands of conversations with parents about health concerns they share about themselves (and their children). The number one concern parents have about their kid's health is when their child gains too much weight from eating too much junk food. Some parents feel helpless to not feed their child(ren) what they ask for and feel guilty later when faced with a doctor telling them that their child(ren) is at risk for being pre-diabetic from their eating habits.

I have encountered many examples of parents asking me for advice about how to improve their health and fitness (as well as that of their children). Many don't know how to prioritize their own exercise or change their eating habits and are confused about how to live a healthy lifestyle. What scares parents more than their own health complications is when their kids start developing diagnoses. When parents hear that their kids need to be on medication, they quickly try to reverse their child's conditions and work to get help. In one example, I've had a parent come to me VERY concerned about their prediabetic 8-year-old child needing to lose weight. They swore they tried everything to get them to lose weight, but nothing seemed to work. After having an initial conversation with the parent and child about how boxing training could help the child lose weight, the parent hired me to do 1-on-1 training for weight loss for their child. The first few weeks went fine, then one Saturday morning, the parent and child slipped back to their old ways of thinking. They were running late to our session, and when they finally arrived at the boxing gym, the child hurried in while eating cupcakes for breakfast. To say the very least, I was shocked and disappointed. I even felt bad for my client because, at that moment, I realized that the progress I was trying to help them make in the boxing gym, was short-lived compared to the influences beyond my control. Jokingly, I had to mention to the parent that their child was supposed to be working on losing weight, not contributing to it. But the parent's excuse for their child eating the cupcakes was that it was the "only" thing the child wanted to eat at the gas station on their way to the boxing gym. Instead of shaming them, I lovingly suggested to the child and parent that eating a banana before training is a better option than cupcakes.

We must collectively, as a society, improve our priorities with physical wellness and our decisions about our food choices. The benefits of parents taking better care of their health are increased energy, less physical pain, and psychological maturity. As a parent, your body has the potential to be vibrant as you age, but you must invest in taking care of it by eating high-nutritional foods, drinking plenty of water, and exercising. It's also what you DON'T do that keeps the body healthy and pain-free. By not feeding it toxins (e.g., smoking, alcohol, fast food, etc.), the potential to have optimal vitality makes doing things as you age more enjoyable. All of us only have one body to use and we can't trade it in and get an upgraded model (like a new car). Parents must learn to prioritize investing in improving their health outcomes not only for themselves but for their children.

Material

Material things are often used as resources that make life more convenient and enjoyable. Parents buy things like clothes, cars, and homes to provide for themselves (and their children) and create a sense of comfort that they can enjoy. Material goods are essential to a person's external well-being and can positively (or negatively) affect a person's mental health. They can positively impact a person's mental health through having a sense of pride in their appearance or negatively impact a person's mental health through jealousy (or overspending habits that create bad debt). Purchasing material things by themselves isn't a bad thing, but a person must be wise in knowing what purchases are worth having in the long run (e.g., assets) and what purchases cause too much bad debt (e.g., liabilities).

People need material goods to support their lifestyles, but they must also be disciplined about what (and how much) they purchase. It takes a mindset of understanding that it is a good thing to have constraints and for parents not to put themselves in debt over temporary pleasures. People often overestimate how happy they think something will make them feel and underestimate how unhappy something can make them feel (after the "honeymoon phase" after purchasing it). When you consider things from that perspective, it should make a person think twice before buying material things whether it will be worth it for them in the long-term or not.

Americans live in a capitalist society where lines of credit allow us to access many material things immediately. Advertisements through marketing on social media and other media outlets (e.g., TV, podcast, radio, etc.) stimulate people to purchase things from their influence. Many people, in turn, fall victim to spending money emotionally and then find themselves in debt trying to afford what they purchased through credit. To avoid getting caught up in buying material things (which can negatively impact one's finances), one must be very disciplined and not emotionally tempted to overspend on what one can't afford. In my opinion, living beyond one's means is NEVER a good idea. It is a great idea for people to strive to improve their financial standing by practicing material maturity through a mindset of longevity.

With all the ways to access credit to purchase material items immediately, parents must learn to be more patient with their spending habits. Instead of falling for their temptations, parents should choose to be less reactionary when purchasing material things that capture their attention. Purchasing material things is like casting votes toward becoming the person you want to be through investing in what you prioritize at the moment. When parents spend money on material possessions, they should always be mindful to try to avoid drowning in bad debt that they can't leverage later if they hit hard times. Material spending directly impacts a parent's wellness, and understanding how their purchasing decisions impact their mental health is a critical factor in their overall wellness.

Community

When thinking about community, what should come to mind is being in a group with like-minded people where you live, work, or regularly vibe around. Being in a community with others is a fantastic way to learn new skills, collaborate with great minds, and pool resources together to improve things for the greater good of the partnership. When you're in the company of great people, you can feed off of each other's energy and come up with great ideas that could help people understand things they may not have thought of by themselves.

In 2020, I was fortunate enough to be asked to serve on the board of directors of Main Street, a nonprofit in Rockville, MD. Main Street is an inclusive community that provides apartment housing and programming for residents who are both adults with disabilities and able-bodied citizens. Main Street was founded by my great friend (Jillian Copeland), who was looking for housing and programming for her son (Nicol) but didn't like the options she initially was looking for where Nicol could thrive.

Ever since Nicol was born, he has faced life-threatening mental and physical disabilities, which have unfortunately caused him to have countless seizures his entire life (he's now 25). Most people don't realize that people who grow up with mental and physical disabilities have a hard time finding jobs throughout their lives, and that leads to a lack of independence as adults.

A critical time for people with mental and physical disabilities is right after graduating from grade school. It is a common experience for the mental and physical disability community and even has a title to describe the social isolation they experience called "falling off the cliff." "Falling off the cliff" means that a person living with "high" disabilities after they graduate from high school usually stays at home with their parents. The parents of mentally and physically disabled citizens, unfortunately, become their children's lifelong caretakers because it's hard for their children to find work. From having fewer employment or programming options to building a lifestyle of their own liking, people with mental and physical disabilities often live in isolation (sometimes for the rest of their lives).

Jillian didn't want that lifestyle for Nicol and wanted him to continue to evolve as a dignified citizen who could contribute to society. When she didn't find anything suitable for his needs, Jillian boldly decided to start her own facility to offer an environment where her son could thrive (not just survive). Since its inception in August 2020, Main Street has been a beckon of life for Nicol and many other families from across the country.

Not only is Main Street a housing facility, but it also offers a variety of programming and activities that offer residents ways to meet and make new friends. However, Main Street isn't just a bubble for people with disabilities, it strives to be a hub for connection to add benefits to the greater community. To encourage inclusivity, it offers memberships for the greater community to attend classes and participate in activities with their residents. I even partnered with Main Street to bring students from my nonprofit, Donte's Boxing & Wellness Foundation (www.DontesFoundation.org), to help my students have good leadership experiences that empower both students and residents. Because Jillian experienced a lack of resources to solve her son's lack of opportunity, she has created a community that helps other families solve similar concerns. The world is a better place because she has solved her son's needs.

This is what community building is all about. When people rally around a common goal to resolve issues, many good things can happen. An old African proverb says, "If you want to go fast, go alone. If you want to go far, go together." When people contribute to communities they feel invested in, it enhances society's greater good and has personal intrinsic value. People should seek out serving others by contributing to issues they feel passionate about and serve others with positive intentions. Being part of a community is a form of wellness through sacrifice, unselfish thinking, and commitment. Whether giving through service, financial donations, or joining advisory boards to help companies with their missions, making an impact through being a part of a community can positively enhance any person's wellness.

Relationships

Forging good relationships is one of the best investments a person can make. They can increase a person's quality of life through sharing resources, enjoying like-minded companionship, and trust. There is also a responsibility factor that comes with forming good relationships. A person (especially parents) should follow a standard code of not lying, cheating, or practicing deceit with others they want to be involved with. Instead, being the type of person who will be sought after to be accountable, dependable, and a resource when needed are good attributes of being somebody anyone would want to be in a relationship with.

Good relationships are best when two parties are honest with their intentions and are genuine in their interactions with each other. Practicing that is a mindset skill that involves living a life of integrity and treating others how you would like to be treated. Anyone who wants to be good in relationships should think about how they can become more selfless through their actions towards others. That involves investing time in adding value to others, being kind (aka - not being a jerk), and remembering (and celebrating) key areas of a person's life (e.g., birthdays, anniversaries, etc.). It is important to be unselfish and show others that they matter by prioritizing their needs at times above your own. It is also important to model to others how a person would like to be treated by treating others how they would like to be treated with the same respect. Those who treat others with respect and civility often get the same in return. A person being their most genuine (and hopefully kind self) will attract other individuals with like characteristics and repel (or replace) those who don't share the same character traits as themselves.

A lot of people who aren't good with relationships are too self-focused on themselves. They make themselves the center of discussion in every conversation and often turn conversations back to their opinion to have the last word about everything. They can be completely unaware that they are "downers" to be around (e.g., complainers), self-absorbed, and lack self-awareness. Basically, they aren't interested in hearing anything other than what they want to say and only pay attention to what they want to hear. They are too narcissistic to take other's feelings and perspectives into consideration, and NEVER believe that they are wrong about anything. They don't ever want (or feel) the need to apologize and are emotionally sensitive to any criticism of themselves. Other traits of people that aren't good to be in a relationship with are:

- People who constantly feel "victimized" when others don't do what they want.
- A person who is always looking to complain about anything they don't like or is always annoyed by something someone else is doing.

- Never feel comfortable hearing different perspectives or other people's points of view.
- Wants to stop listening to others whenever they are challenged with something they don't agree with.

To create good relationships, you must be honest with those whom you interact with. It is non-negotiable to be willing to learn different perspectives, communicate openly about your perspectives (without being too judgmental), and seek to listen to what others have to say. There are right and wrong ways to treat people in relationships. A person who treats a person right is truthful in their dealings with others, has integrity with their character by not cheating them, and does unto others as they would want them to do unto them. However, people who behave disrespectfully, have ill will toward or actively work against the better interest of a person's well-being, and are horrendous people to avoid at all costs.

A person should always strive to be the kind of friend they would want to be in a relationship with. That starts by treating others with civility and respect, plus looking out for people to see them do well for themselves. When people realize that relationships start with who they are, they can make the right adjustments to model the actions they want to receive from others in return. When people focus on holding themselves accountable for their behavior, treating others with civility, and aligning their intentions for good outcomes, they breed a good reputation that will attract like-minded people. Relationships are a key factor in a person's wellness, and being able to master your attitude and mindset will be a determining factor in attracting others you prefer to be in relationships with.

Getting Your "D.I.E.T" Right!

Getting your diet right involves more than just what a person eats. It also involves what people watch on screens, what music they listen to, and even who they spend time with. All of these factors impact how a person lives on a daily basis and can impact their mental health directly (and indirectly). When I think about what a diet represents, it embodies what you ingest physically, mentally, and spiritually. I came up with an acronym to break down how I best describe what a "D.I.E.T" represents to me:

D - Dietary Behaviors
I – Information Intake
E – Entertainment Pursuits
T – Thought Training

*Below, I will describe how each topic influences your personal outcomes and why it is so important to correct them to become your best self.

D - Dietary behaviors

First off, people LOVE FOOD! Since we were kids, we have been given food from people who love us as a way to show that they care about our wellbeing. As babies, our parents put our food on a spoon and made airplane noises, then made flight maneuvers to get our eyes to follow that imaginary plane until it crashed inside our mouths. We have since carried that same enjoyment into our adulthoods, and food is STILL looked at as a "fun" adventure that we should celebrate. We have been raised to eat certain foods out of tradition, scheduled to eat at the same time every day (breakfast, lunch, and dinner), and are teased daily with marketing for fast and junk food ads on TV. We cannot escape food (nor should we), but we should take more stock of how we are treating our health through our food choices that impact our personal longevity.

We often eat what we are used to out of habit from how we were raised. Whether we fix food the way our parents taught us how to prepare it or order it off the menu from a restaurant, we like food the way we are used to eating it. Even when holidays or traditions occur, we "automatically" think about eating certain foods for the occasion. When we think about Thanksgiving, we think about turkey, mac and cheese, sweet potatoes, stuffing, and more. When we go out to see a movie, we want to eat popcorn (and/or candy) and drink a soda. If we want to celebrate a birthday, everybody celebrates by eating cake and ice cream. Even in the suburbs, it is a tradition that every Friday night is "Pizza Night," and families stay home to watch a movie together. These options are so embedded in us, so much so that we don't even question them.

As a boxing coach, I talk to people ALL THE TIME about food. Many people come to me for many different reasons, but the majority of adults come to train with me for weight loss concerns. For many people, food has always been a "weakness," and they struggle to keep a healthy weight as they get older. Eating healthier has always been a challenge for most people because bland foods are less desirable than the sugary taste of junk foods. Often, people wait until they have a reason to eat healthier before prioritizing eating healthier options (specifically for weight loss). Personally, I have seen a lot of family, friends, clients, and students suffer tremendous health consequences (mostly because of their eating habits). Some of those people have suffered going blind or have had their leg amputated from having diabetes. Others have had heart attacks and strokes. Unfortunately, I see way too many people coming to me to correct their gluttony after a weekend binge of going out, drinking too much, and eating a bunch of junk. Then by Monday morning, wanting me to "kick their butt" from the damage they did to themselves. All of the weekend festivities, holidays, and birthdays add up overtime, and thinking long-term can help avoid a lot of negative outcomes from becoming realities.

To change the current forecast of negative health projections, more people should share real-life stories of health scares to inform others how serious health outcomes can feel. For example, I had a case when a guy came into the boxing gym right after his doctor's appointment and was in a panic to get in shape. His doctor had just told him that he was one point shy of being diabetic and that he needed to start exercising right away to get his numbers down. In a panic about not wanting to take insulin for the rest of his life, he went to multiple gyms on his way home (and my gym was one of the places he stopped by). We had a very frank conversation, and the guy decided to sign up to train with me that same week. He ended up losing over one hundred pounds and trained with me for over three years.

Unfortunately, it took that former client that extreme awareness before he was motivated to get himself in better shape. The sad part is he is one of the MANY examples I see on a weekly basis, and it is becoming more frequent every year. When people continuously make bad health choices like eating low-nutrition foods and drinks, they are bound to take many medications for high blood pressure and pills to help their bodies regulate themselves. By paying more attention to dietary intake, people can take proactive measures to avoid bad health outcomes. It shouldn't take until people are almost forced to be on medications for the rest of their lives or need to undergo expensive surgeries to become more thoughtful about their health. Instead, emphasis needs to be placed on the benefits of healthy living and preventive lifestyles, which can help save people a lot of pain and more costly expenses.

I – Information Intake

What a person ingests goes beyond what they eat. It is also the kind of information they consume, the news they watch, and the podcasts they like to listen to that can influence their mental state. Whatever external sources anybody chooses to be influenced by should be based on the type of person they want to become. Some people may think it's not that serious to pay close attention to everything you listen to or watch, but those sources become backdrops to what you think about throughout your day. A case in point: Have you ever listened to a song on your way to school or work, and the last song you heard stayed in your mind for the rest of the day? I have! That is the power of letting what you give your attention to become a part of you. What a person is directly (or indirectly) influenced by "feeds" their minds and impacts their thinking for better or worse.

We often believe that the background noise playing in our rooms, offices, or car rides doesn't affect our mindset (but it does). For instance, what news channels we watch (e.g., Fox News, CNN, etc.) can seep into our subconscious and create a bias toward how we view events happening domestically and abroad. We take those soundbites and include them in our conversations, they influence our decision-making, and impact our points of view. Historically, we, as American citizens, have trusted what we have seen on TV (especially news channels) and have allowed them to be like the gospel of our shared realities. Lately, however, our formerly trusted ways of being informed have eroded trust, and people have become more skeptical about the information presented to broadcast.

As a society, we must do more background research to explore what sources we get our information from and ensure that what we consume is actually factual. Moving forward, we must do more "fact-checking" ourselves to ensure that television, radio (or podcast), and social media are presenting us with actual information that is truthful. By being more diligent about our media consumption, we can improve our consciousness and become more mature citizens. Media can be a great resource of information when used to educate and raise awareness. By making more of an effort to become knowledgeable about how those mediums influence our subconscious, we can learn to be more mindful of the impact of what we use to inform ourselves.

E – Entertainment pursuits

Everybody has their preference of how they like to "unwind." Whether you like sports, news shows, reality TV, video games, or movies, all are powerful portals that can impact a person's awareness. Leisure activities have powerful influences on a person's psyche and can influence people in small and big ways. Entertainment has such a powerful influence on our subconscious, that we sometimes subtly reenact (and use sayings) what we learn from what we hear and watch. Whether it's commercial jingles like McDonald's theme "I'm lovin' it" or rap music that is "catchy" that people party to, our entertainment pursuits can be contagious.

We have all grown up and watched certain TV shows and movies that have impacted our lives. Whether watching a TV show like "Martin" or a movie like "Mean Girls," they made many people relate to the realities of the characters they saw being portrayed on screen. Specifically, the power of TV shows and movies can even impact the representation of how people see themselves (and others). Based on the actions of the characters being played, roles seen on screen create stereotypes and biases through how characters are presented.

When people tend to see their race and gender identified through media, it makes an impression on how they see themselves (for better or worse). It even makes an impression on others who may not interact very often (or not at all) with other races or genders. Representation matters on screen because it creates a perception about what people should say (and/or do) when communicating with others. Sometimes, people take what they initially see on screen as a reference to reenact what they saw in their real lives without even realizing it. Entertainment pursuits entrance its audiences in ways that give framing to life's situations and impact how we, in turn, use them as ways to see our own lives. As humans, we are impressionable much more than we think, and we must become much more aware of our weakness of mimicking what we give our attention to.

T – Thought training

Thoughts are like a powerful fuel that energizes a person's actions. What type of fuel a person uses depends on what motivates them. Some people are fueled by buying things that inspire them or doing something positive for someone else, while others are fueled by hate and gain energy from the drama they emit. A lot of our thoughts come from our subconscious, which comes from the people we surround ourselves with, the environments we roam in, and what we give our attention to. If parents can get their thoughts to be positive examples of how to think, that rubs off on their child(ren) and everyone else around them.

Thought training is all about improving decision-making and achieving the results a person wants to feel proud of. Thoughts are powerful, and a person can speak their future reality into existence. How we repeatedly talk to ourselves becomes a prophecy over our destiny. The way we talk to ourselves can affect our confidence, how we deal with our emotions, and how we make decisions.

When parents want to practice getting better at improving their thoughts throughout the day, it is important to practice positive self-talk because we will always make mistakes, and how we view those mistakes can help us learn lessons and improve ourselves. Instead of being quick to be harsh (or even dismissive) of our flaws, we should be willing to disrupt negative thinking and replace those thoughts with a calm, assertive focus on learning lessons from our mistakes. When people practice good decision-making, they feel proud of themselves because they got the results they wanted to achieve.

By parents learning to master their own thoughts, they become better leaders who can understand not only themselves but also others as well. While it can be difficult to reach a consensus within a person's mind, being able to successfully overcome distractions to create positive outcomes is an admirable skill. By their example, how parents treat themselves through the way they make decisions models how their children perceive them. Therefore, when parents can get their thought processes to be in line with their values, they can instill those virtues in their children by leading by example.

Why should parents care about how well they lead themselves?

By all accounts, parents feel like they are doing a good job raising their kids the best way they know how. So, why should they bother to be concerned about how they're living (and does that affect their kids)? The short answer is "YES!!!" Parents are the first representation of leadership that their kids experience in their lives. They play a vital role in establishing the foundation and outlook in which their child(ren) will learn the ways of the world. What parents say, how they behave, what they reprimand (and allow in their presence) will all impact their children's standards for the rest of their lives.

The question, "Should parents care about how well they lead

themselves?" is one that should be easy to answer. What would you say if someone asked you this question and substituted it with any other authority figure? "Should teachers care about how well they lead themselves?" "Should pastors or priests care about how well they lead themselves?" "Should Presidents care about how well they lead themselves?" The answer to every authority figure should be "YES!" Every authority figure should be held accountable to the highest standards possible and set an example for those behind them to follow.

Kids pay a lot of attention to what they see and quickly pick up on what is acceptable in the environments they enter. Since parents are the ultimate authority figures in their kid's lives, how they live around their child(ren) makes a lasting impression. Even the smallest mistake can cause a child to remember what a parent said (or did), which could impact that child for the rest of their life. Every interaction a parent has with their child(ren) matters and creates patterns that resonate with their child(ren) subconsciously. How a parent displays patience (or the lack thereof), the attitude they have around their child(ren), and how they allow their child(ren) to talk to them form how their child(ren) will behave when they go out in the "real world." Parents can't afford to take their positions in their kid's lives for granted because EVERYTHING a parent does impacts their child(ren) while in their presence.

Parents should care about how well they lead themselves because they are giving permission to their child(ren) to act the same way they do by their example. The role of a parent is to be a model citizen who should demonstrate by their example how their child(ren) could similarly grow up to lead their own lives. When parents don't care about how well they live, their child(ren) lacks examples to model after and has a harder time adjusting to understanding themselves and society. It is VERY important that parents live their lives by being positive role models because their kids use their example in how they conduct themselves through their parent's mindset, attitudes, and behaviors.

T.I.P.S. (T-Takeaways / Insights / Perspectives / Stories)

T.I.P.S. is to help the reader remember at least three things before moving on to the next chapter. Throughout this chapter, I have made points to help parents be more aware of how they can better lead themselves and be the example they want their children to follow. We have discussed three primary sets of practices that parents can do to become their best selves. Those three primary sets of practices are:

- The 7 Self-Mastery practices: R-Routine / A-Action / A-Adaptation / D-Decisions / D-Discipline / G-Goals / F-Faith
- The 5 Wellness Practices
- Getting your "D.I.E.T." right!

The 7 Basic Self-Mastery Focuses uses the acronym "RAADD GF" (aka Raadd Girl Friend") to help a person remember a system of thought. Those acronyms stand for R-Routine / A-Action / A-Adaptation / D-Decisions / D-Discipline / G-Goals / F-Faith.

Routine – Establishing routines is great for creating habits to work towards changing behaviors.

Action – Action produces merits and ways to see (and earn) progress.

Adaption – Learning how to adapt helps make less awkward engagements, enhances experiences, and lessens stress.

Decisions – Decisions help focus a person's mind to work toward a desired result.

Discipline - Discipline helps train a person's mind to do mundane things that they don't want to do but do anyway like they would love to do them (with a good attitude).

Goals – Having goals is the inspiration that helps aim a person towards a desired result.

Faith – Faith creates a feeling of confidence (and optimism) to overcome hesitation and doubts.

"The 5 Wellness Practices":

These five practices include:

* Financial
* Physical
* Material
* Community
* Relationships

Financial – Financial literacy should be more central to Western cultural teachings and taught from early childhood education to college. Unfortunately, since financial literacy isn't taught in schools, people must make extra efforts to educate themselves through reading books, listening to podcasts, and researching on the Internet. It's not a common thought to consider financial literacy a wellness factor, but it's as essential as any other area of wellness from a financial standpoint. Finances influence what you can afford to eat, your healthcare access, physiological stress, and other important wellness factors.

Physical – Making physical fitness a high priority is essential for enjoying many life experiences. Investing in the upkeep of your physical well-being through exercising and eating high-nutritious foods is a way to prolong life and be a parent for as long as possible. When people prioritize their physical abilities, it improves them psychologically, increases vitality, prevents multiple diseases, and so much more. If parents don't keep up with themselves physically well, the alternatives are they will experience many physical pains, will need to take medications to stabilize their bodily functions, will increase the probability of having surgeries to fix health complications, and more. Taking a more preventative approach to self-care is more cost-efficient, improves life enjoyment, and increases personal confidence.

Material—Material things can be assets or liabilities. Understanding the value of assets (things that can be held or appreciated in value) is wise. Good assets include buying real estate, certain Swiss watches, or even some paintings (e.g., Salvator Mundi by Leonardo da Vinci, etc.). Likewise, understanding liabilities (materials that depreciate after purchase) is like buying most cars, clothes, or shoes. Learning the differences between assets and liabilities is important, as it creates awareness and helps people develop better spending habits.

Community – Being part of a community is an important aspect of wellness because it creates a base of social support and resources in times of need. Being in a community enhances self-worth, creates a sense of belonging, and allows one to unite with others to bring about change. The earlier story about how Jillian Copeland created Main Street to help her son Nicol (and other families looking for a disability-friendly residence) is an excellent example of creating a community. The inclusiveness of Main Street has had a tremendous impact on the lives of the residents there. The testimonies of people who say, "They feel safe" and that "Main Street is like a refuge of joy" speak volumes.

It shows how being a part of a community can be a testament to wellness, which is good for a person's mental and physical health.

Relationships - Picking the right people in your life is essential. Who you decide to marry, what kind of people you choose to hang around, and even the kinds of people you frequently interact with all matter to your wellness. People who have access to you can influence your moods, behavior, and priorities (so choose wisely).

Getting your "D.I.E.T." right: D-Dietary Behaviors / I-Information Intake / E-Entertainment Pursuits / T-Thought Training.

D-Dietary Behaviors

It is no secret that people LOVE food. But what you eat affects your physical and mental well-being in more ways than one. As a boxing coach, I have spent YEARS trying to get people to improve their food choices. I have experienced so much "pushback" with clients and students because they have been conditioned to eat certain foods in specific environments (e.g., movies, birthday parties, etc.). It is hard for people to change how they were raised, and most just accept that they are going to do what they want to do (regardless of the consequences).

People are addicted to the taste of junk and fast foods, and the allure seems too great for most to overcome. Factors such as what people ate as kids influence their eating habits as adults, and who people hang around as adults influence their food choices as well. People have been so conditioned by the way they've been raised by their parent's food habits that it's very difficult for them to opt out of what they have been used to eating their whole lives. To try to change the traditional ways most people choose to eat, they must be taught more information on how eating fewer nutritional foods (and drinks) negatively affects their bodies. People must have the maturity to decide not to continue consuming foods that cause negative health consequences and to practice replacing those disease-causing foods with foods that will help them live lives of less pain and suffering.

People tend to eat foods with less nutritional value in excess without REALLY thinking about how it truly affects them over time. The trick to eating healthier is to think about how your "future self" will feel beyond the immediate gratification of eating junk foods. Think about whether you would feel prouder of yourself later in the day when you don't feel bloated (and maybe feel the need to take Pepto-Bismol to settle your stomach). If a person doesn't want to feel that, they should resist the temptation to eat those junk foods and listen to their "inner voice" telling them it's not worth it. Foods that parents should strive to instill in their intake are foods that give them more lasting energy (e.g., smoothies, etc.) and foods that are preferable to stay away from sap a person's energy after consumption (e.g., fast foods, etc.).

I-Information Intake

What we ingest is more than what we put in our mouths to eat and drink. Everything that we allow into our consciousness affects our well-being. Whether it's what news sources we listen to or what movies and TV shows we watch, what we give our attention to affects our mentality, mood, and attitude. Being mindful of what we focus on can boost our energy or decrease our mindset based on its influence on our lives. This awareness also applies to hanging out with certain people. Whether it's listening, watching, or being entertained, our focused attention seeps into our subconscious and can impact our mentality in various uncomplimentary ways (e.g., bad attitude, worrying, gossiping, etc.).

E-Entertainment Pursuits

When people want to relax, they want to do something to take their minds off work (or whatever stress is on their minds). What most people call "downtime," which is used as "wasting" time watching and listening to information that doesn't improve a person's well-being, can (and should be) better utilized to improve a person. "Downtime" should be reframed as "High Time" to help a person steadily work towards becoming a better version of themselves. Using "High Time" to take accountability towards improving oneself should be preferred. To improve a person's odds of becoming a better version of themselves, I suggest watching programming in their "High Time" that helps improve themselves towards being the type of person they want to become. Spending time researching areas of knowledge about a subject to increase a person's awareness gives them a "blueprint" for becoming a better version of themselves. I believe that the best way people can enhance their value is by using every moment possible to become better versions of themselves. By using "High Time" to replace "downtime," a person can utilize their time wisely to work towards learning, developing ideas, and working on projects they want to pursue.

T-Thought Training

Training your thoughts to work for you (instead of against

you) is a skill. When your mental dialogue gets too emotional or distracted, you must talk back to your thoughts to disrupt negative statements that aren't motivating you toward your goals. As parents, getting better at training your thoughts are about choosing to be more mature for your future self (and your kids). By parents constantly recalibrating positive self-talk in their thoughts, they can become better emotionally, be more confident, and become more mature examples for their child(ren). It also helps them accomplish goals that they want to achieve.

Thought training is a combination of all the "D.I.E.T." acronyms combined. What you eat can affect your physical capabilities and focus. What news information you listen to can impact you for better or for worse. What entertainment you spend "High Time" on subconsciously influences your thoughts. When parents can master their thought processes to accomplish goals that are hard to achieve, they become blueprint creators that their child(ren) can model after. Learning to overcome distractions and negative thinking is a skill that will enhance concentration while also increasing the ability of a parent relationally to connect with their children.

CHAPTER 3:
GETTING YOUNGER GENERATIONS TO BE MORE PREPARED FOR ADULTHOOD.

In Chapter 1, I discussed the impact of "Butler Parenting" on children's mental health. The call to action was to help parents understand how their behaviors affect their children and what they can do about it. Chapter 2 provided tips on how parents can improve themselves, such as "The 5 Wellness Practices," "The 7 Basic Self-Mastery Focuses," and "D.I.E.T." Those topics emphasized ways that parents can hold themselves accountable while also becoming better leaders for their children. The third and final chapter focuses on raising awareness among parents (and other authority figures) to help educate younger generations to become more prepared for adulthood. I suggest that parents take the initiative to discuss adulthood responsibilities with their children (even those as young as elementary grades) so that younger generations can be better prepared for their future.

Most young people have NO CLUE about what it takes to be an adult. I believe it's essential to have more open discussions about topics like taxes and aging, as they are often considered taboo and not adequately addressed. Having discussions about these inevitable realities is important, and many aspects of "adulting" should be taught to younger generations before they grow older. There are many stages of adulthood that younger generations should be aware of, but I have chosen to address three key areas that I believe are fundamental to address in adulthood called "The 3 Adulting Awarenesses." These areas of adulting are Finance, Health, and Life Skills. By addressing these three areas, parents (and other authority figures) can better guide younger generations as they transition to adulthood.

As adults, we are all too familiar with the time-consuming responsibilities of adulting. We have to manage the life we have built and are constantly playing "catch-up" to handle all of our obligations and choices. Younger generations often have NO CLUE about what it takes to truly take care of themselves (independently) without their parent's assistance. I believe that providing younger generations with early education about adulting can bring hope and optimism. This is not only for future generations but also for parents who worry about their children's ability to live independently as adults. The sooner that younger generations can learn how to prepare for adulting, the better off they will be for their future.

"The 3 Adulting Awarenesses" addresses subjects that parents (and other authority figures) can help educate younger generations about adulting. As parents, you should want your kids to learn how to be independent and handle their own responsibilities. These "3 Adulting Awarenesses" are topics aimed at creating a dialog about the realities younger generations will face as adults in the "real world." Below is an outline for "The 3 Adulting Focuses", which are the main subjects of the rest of the chapter. I will break down each topic to help parents address important subjects that I believe could help their child(ren) become more prepared for adulthood.

The 3 Adulting Awarenesses are:

(1) Finances

- Bills (e.g., phone, healthcare, credit card, car payment, etc.)
- Housing
- Taxes
- Investing
- What are assets and liabilities?
- Credit

(2) Health

- Wellness Practices (like working out or playing sports, knowledge of food choices, "What is food?")
- Aging

(3) Life Skills

- Work Ethics/Habits
- Communicating
- Networking
- Relationships
- Learning Current Events
- Sports

The 1st Adulting Awareness: Finances

Discussing finances with younger generations is vital because financial literacy can significantly impact their future options, decisions, and quality of life. By not teaching youth the importance of financial literacy, we, as adults, are doing a drastic disservice to the future well-being of youth in America (and elsewhere across the world). It is imperative to educate youth about managing bills, housing costs, taxes, investing, credit, and other financial matters. Talking with younger generations about finances shows parents care about their children's future well-being and helps them build financial confidence. Instead of feeling awkward about discussing money matters with their children, parents should view it as an opportunity to demonstrate concern for their future independence as adults.

Many young people are often unaware of the cost of everyday things that they take for granted. They usually don't know how much bills such as internet, cell phone services, utilities (e.g., electricity, gas, water, etc.), and rent or mortgage payments actually amount to. A lot of youth act like what they use is "free" because they aren't used to paying for them. Younger generations have been spoiled to believe that access to things is easy to come by purely because they haven't had to labor themselves to afford those luxuries. Without experiences having to contribute to the access to resources they use, younger generations don't fully realize that hard work is the cost of affording their access to resources. Youth need more exposure to financial realities and discussions about the costs (and sacrifices) of affording their luxuries. These discussions should be an open dialogue that shows how much basic utilities cost and educates young people about affording resources in a nonjudgemental way.

During my conversations with kids at schools and in the boxing gym, I often emphasize to my students the importance of increasing their knowledge in order to improve their earning potential. When I asked them questions about how much they think it will cost to live independently (and pay their own bills), many of them have no idea. I regularly share details about my own expenses, explaining the cost of each bill and emphasizing that many of them are a fixed amount each month. Some students are surprised by the expenses and express concern about how they will be able to afford to pay them in the future.

Many parents do not talk to their kids about money, assuming that they will learn about finances as they grow older. This lack of communication often leads to younger generations not understanding how to earn money and manage it. They end up seeing money as something to spend rather than something to earn, save, and invest for the future. Without teaching young people about financial awareness, it will be harder for them to achieve financial independence as adults.

Recently, some high schools have started implementing programs and courses on financial literacy. Hopefully, youth will learn useful information that they can apply to better their financial future. Besides schools, it's crucial for parents to take the lead in educating their children about real-life expenses (and financial responsibilities). Family conversations about finances can be made during everyday activities such as car rides and meals together (or they can be planned in advance). It's essential for younger generations to learn about earning and managing money, whether through school, conversations at home, or government programs. Financial literacy should be a mandatory part of all school curriculums and a priority for all parents in educating their children (as it forms the foundation of independence in a capitalist society).

Bills

When it comes to bills, younger generations need as much education to help them learn about their potential monthly responsibilities as possible. Paying bills are a big part of being an adult and it's essential for young people to understand the different types of bills, their average costs, and how often they need to be paid. Talking to younger generations about bills shouldn't be daunting but rather seen as an opportunity to connect with them on a personal level.

These conversations can be a bit "awkward" and lack comfort for some, but they are needed discussions to help younger generations mature into their adulthood. These initial conversations should take place in settings where you can discuss the use of money, how to earn it, and how to budget for expenses. Many individuals prefer not to discuss their personal finances with anyone (including their children) and feel that talking about money is too formal and strict. However, it is important to take the initiative to educate young people to become more financially educated, so that they can establish financial literacy before adulting. If parents avoid discussing financial literacy, it can delay their child's (ren's) ability to be proficient when they become independent. Having these discussions is an act of love that helps younger generations learn how to handle their financial responsibilities, and it creates core teachings that can last a lifetime.

When discussing adulthood financial responsibilities with my students, I often use real-life examples to make the topic more relatable. For instance, previously, I've shared a few examples of how much certain bills cost to run my boxing gym. Some of the costs were monthly expenses like electricity ($300), gym lease ($3,000), high-speed internet plus phone ($250), among others. The usual feedback I get is, "That's expensive!" Using real-life examples makes talking about bills more urgent, and younger generations start to think about how they will be able to afford those costs when they get older. This approach helps them understand that adulthood comes with significant financial responsibilities, and they need to be prepared for these when they reach that stage in their lives.

Discussions about bills can't be emphasized enough. For youth to survive as adults within a Western civilization, they should be educated about what to expect when living independently. Parents should initiate more conversations about how much expenses cost (and how to pay for them). Financial education should be introduced to younger generations at a very early age (ideally in elementary grades) to help them learn how to earn money, budget, make investments, and take responsibility for their finances. When younger generations are exposed to the realities of money at an early age, they are usually better equipped to handle their financial responsibilities as adults.

Housing

Younger generations should be more aware of home ownership (or even renting) before they become adults. Many kids have no idea about the requirements for getting a home, including the bills and maintenance involved. Information about how much a down payment is needed to own a home, what a mortgage is, and what home equity is about is all too important to share with younger generations. Independent responsibilities are vast when becoming an adult, and they should be given priority in educating young people about them because they are overwhelmingly tough to deal with in adulthood.

Whether younger generations will rent or own a home, modern-day parents (and other adults) should prepare youth to learn what it will be like to live independently. They should share information about renting an apartment, including typical requirements such as providing the first and last month's rent as a deposit before signing the lease. Or, when wanting to buy a house, having to have the astronomical amount upfront to make a down payment (e.g., $51,250, $130,800, etc.) can be overwhelming for most people. These are basic understandings that most people don't know until they get older, then scramble to figure out how to do them on their own. This should be common knowledge BEFORE youth might need a place to lease or purchase as an adult.

Younger generations also need to understand how having a good credit score will help them access housing. That's a big factor because it can decide whether or not they could be approved to qualify as tenants (or for a mortgage loan). It also plays a part in how much a tenant could get charged or the mortgage interest rate (depending on what their credit score is). When younger generations understand that they could even be denied access to live in a property because they could be seen as a potential bad tenant (or too much of a loan risk), they realize that having good credit is very important when it comes to housing. Understanding credit is so important that I created a whole section dedicated to the subject later in this chapter.

Getting housing to live in is one thing, but affording the responsibilities of paying bills and utilities is another. Youth should also be taught to factor in all the other expenses associated with living on their own as well. Information like mortgages or rent, different home insurances (e.g., HVAC, flood, property, etc.), and utilities (e.g., cable/internet, electricity, gas, etc.) are monthly, quarterly, or annual bills that are factors in renting or owning a home. Whether it's monthly bills that come at the same time every month (with their varying or fixed costs) or preparing for unexpected emergencies (through insurance or saving for them in a budget), younger generations need a lot more education on these awarenesses.

Owning (or renting) a home is one of the most important responsibilities a person will have. A key aspect of living independently is affording all of the expenses associated with a home. Parents should educate their children about leasing options, mortgages, credit, and bills, so they can learn about housing costs at an early age. When younger generations are more familiar with the costs they will face as adults, they can improve their chances of sustaining their independence.

Taxes

Taxes are a hard sell for any parent to help their child(ren) understand. It's hard to discuss taxes because it's like describing having a bill that charges you for using a service (or buying an item), but it doesn't "feel" like it benefits you directly. The underlying education about taxes is that it helps pay for general services that the general public shares. Tax revenue covers things like military protection, the Transportation Security Administration /TSA (also known as "the airports" in America), public streetlights, and so on. Conversing with younger generations about taxes can be challenging for them to understand, but it is educational for them to learn about how taxes can impact their lives.

When I talk to my students about taxes, I usually tell them that there are three basic ways to think about taxes in America. Taxes are typically collected on what you own, earn, and buy. For example, property tax is an annual tax charged on the value of your home. Income tax (depending on where you live) is an annual tax, and sales tax is a charge when buying goods and services. Trying to explain this to younger generations helps them see the differences between taxes and breaks down the financial responsibilities they may have to bear.

We often take for granted many services funded by taxes. Services such as road maintenance, public education, and the legal system are all possible with government funding. If parents took the time to discuss taxes with their child(ren), they might become interested in how taxes could be used to better their lives and society as a whole. The potential of younger generations having an interest in taxes could result in better due diligence with how funding is spent. Not only that, but electing politicians who would better govern the spending of the funds to improve communities within their jurisdictions (including becoming good politicians themselves).

As a child, I had NO IDEA how much taxes would affect my life as an adult. It wasn't until I started getting a paycheck that I would ask my parents and friends, "Why is so much of what I work for going towards taxes?" Until then, I didn't know about social security, Medicaid, or federal income taxes. That's why I'm such an advocate for educating younger generations about taxes! I don't want others to be as surprised as I was because of not being aware of what to expect.

My "real" introduction to taxes came when I started working a salary job as a teacher. During my first year of teaching, I also worked extra hours coaching and doing after-care. A year later, when my tax accountant informed me that "I made too much money.", I was like, "Huh?" All the work that I did grossed my income into another tax bracket, and I had to pay thousands of dollars more in taxes because I didn't have many deductions. It was puzzling when he told me I owed more towards my tax debt because I wasn't aware of tax brackets. I was always told that if you work hard, you can save money and become rich. So, I thought that all a person needed to do was work hard and save their money, and the person could make a good life for themselves. I had NO IDEA how taxes could deduct a person's income. That awakened me to want to learn more about taxes and act on my frustration to understand how to save money.

I was so frustrated from feeling like I had worked all those extra jobs for nothing that I began asking questions to figure out how to become financially well off. I asked my tax accountant, "How can I become rich if every time I make more money, I have to give up more money to the government? That doesn't make sense to me?" Then, he gave me a piece of advice that changed my life forever. He told me, "There are three ways that you can get your taxes down next year. One, you can buy a bigger home, and paying the higher interest on your mortgage would be a tax write-off; two, you can have a child and have a lot of deductions from that; or three, you can start a business." That last part interested me the most, and it was the reason why I became an entrepreneur.

Information needs to be shared with younger generations to prepare them for the realities they will face in the future. We all want younger generations to get good educations, get good jobs, and, in turn, provide for themselves. But the information about what to do AFTER you get the job is just as important (or more) as getting the money itself. Adults should educate younger generations about tax obligations BEFORE paying for them and becoming alarmed by how much they could owe for their contributions.

These are sobering conversations and aren't that much "fun" to talk to kids about, but it is a way to help younger generations learn and be ready for the realities of adulthood. Taking the time to help youth learn about taxes, what gets taken out of their paycheck (e.g., social security, federal, local, etc.), and how to create tax deductions is beneficial to their future. Taxes are a mandatory expense in a capitalistic society. We as adults (especially parents) should educate younger generations about the pros and cons of taxes as early as possible. When we do so, they can be more prepared to learn how their contributions can help the greater society and work to their benefit.

What are assets and liabilities?

Younger generations should learn what assets and liabilities are and the differences between them as early as possible. Assets are valuable property owned by a person (or company) that can be used to pay for debts or used as collateral. Assets can be good investments because they can gain value through appreciation from owning (and maintaining) them. Some good examples of assets are land, stocks, home ownership, Swiss watches (e.g., Rolex, Patek Philippe, IWC, etc.), rare artwork, and some rare purses (like Birkin bags). Investing in good assets is a great way to compound your money through the property you own, which will increase your net worth on a balance sheet.

However, liabilities are usually considered something that a person (or company) owes. Certain ways of obtaining liabilities are usually through borrowings, such as credit card debt, bank loans, mortgage loans, and even car loans. But all liabilities aren't bad. Liabilities can be "Good debt" if used to buy income-producing assets that help you gain more financial benefits (e.g., using home equity to purchase another property, etc.). For example, if a person takes out home equity from their current home for $100,000 and puts it towards buying another property for $500,000 to rent to tenants, then that home equity loan can be used as a "good debt." However, accumulating "bad debt" is like spending money on items that yield low to no returns (e.g., clothes, laptops, cars, etc.). "Bad debt" is considered purchasing a resource that will decrease in value after the initial purchase.

Educating younger generations about assets and liabilities is all about showing them how they impact them and their future. When they can understand how purchasing "bad debt" loses value after they buy it, they will most likely not want to purchase those goods as much as they would like to. Information like that influences purchasing decisions, which helps a person prioritize making better financial decisions for their future.

Most modern-day youth are really into learning about how to earn money and ways to understand how to purchase what they want. They don't really understand the benefits of assets and the complexity of liabilities but should learn about how the values of what they purchase will increase or decrease after they buy them. In the past, I have used class time in the boxing gym to ask my students if they knew anything about assets and liabilities and then explain the differences to them. In part, I would share an example of when I purchased an asset (like a Swiss watch) and how the value of it grew after I purchased it by thousands of dollars. I would do this not to brag but to educate my students through my accomplishments and how they make me feel. It "hits" differently when somebody who's done something can use themselves as examples to make a point.

Parents, school systems, and other adults should educate younger generations about how to think about money and how what they buy could benefit or deteriorate their financial future. Explaining to younger generations how to become financially literate is beneficial to their future so that they won't experience debt crises that can destroy their finances in adulthood. If, as a child, I had known about the differences between assets and liabilities, I would have been much more financially advanced in my adulthood. I would have chosen to save money to purchase more assets than liabilities and become more of a savvy consumer. If you are a parent, coach, or any influence in a child's life, please take time to educate youth on the best practices you know about improving their financial literacy. Their future will depend on it.

Credit

Parents have a significant role in teaching their child(ren) about credit. The impact of credit is vast and multifaceted, as it can have a major effect on a person's life in adulthood. It can determine gaining access to more resources or being denied credit for not paying back owed money. Helping younger generations learn about the importance of having credit as an adult means explaining its pros and cons. Some of the pros are having more access to money to purchase resources upfront and the convenience of not spending all of a person's money all at once. Some of the cons of not having access to credit are not having opportunities to buy access to goods and services and lower options for advancement. Access to credit provides better opportunities for a high standard of living (which requires a lot of resources) and costs more than the average person can afford. These include a college degree, a car, a house, and so much more. Since most people don't have the money upfront to pay for those resources, obtaining a loan (or credit) provides access to them.

Discussions about credit should start at an early age, even before children can apply for credit at 18. Parents should take the lead in explaining to their child(ren) what credit is, its purpose, and how to use it responsibly when they become adults. Young people need to know why having good credit is important because the consequences (and benefits) are too important to leave up to chance. The instant gratification of Western culture influences people to spend money recklessly and not be financially responsible. That creates a mindset that causes people to use credit for quick access and slowly try to pay back a lender in smaller payments over time (with interest). As a person tries to pay back their debt, if the agreed amount isn't paid on time, it can cause the borrower to default on their payments (leaving the lender to impose pre-agreed upon penalties). Those who don't pay back their debts on time are penalized by compounding interest, having a lower credit score, and having higher debt.

As young people grow up, they will likely want to own more expensive things and take on more financial responsibilities. When individuals turn 18 and can get a credit card, they might make a lot of mistakes if they don't fully understand how to use credit cards properly (especially for new college students). I bring up college because credit card companies often try to sign up new college students at the start of the school year, which can be seen as predatory lending. When college students first experience living on campus (or "off campus") for the first time, they quickly experience how expensive it is to live on their own. The temptation to have money on demand becomes enticing, and getting a credit card can be very convenient and come in handy. If young people don't know how credit works, they can end up with a lot of debt very quickly and find themselves in financial trouble as soon as they become adults. Therefore, parents need to talk to their kids about how to use credit responsibly because it's a crucial part of becoming a responsible adult. Managing credit, whether it's college loans, car loans, mortgages, or credit cards, can create financial difficulties that are difficult to afford to pay back and can wreck purchasing power for years to come. Younger generations should be educated on credit as early as elementary grades so that they won't make bad decisions when they are responsible for handling their finances as adults.

The 2nd Adulting Awareness: Health

There is an epidemic of childhood obesity in America, which, in my opinion, is not receiving enough attention. In 2024, I came across an online article stating that over 1 out of 5 children between the ages of 6-11 are obese, and almost 1 out of 4 children between the ages of 12-19 are obese (according to the CDC / https://www.cdc.gov/obesity/data/childhood.html). This is a concerning issue that many parents are dealing with, and they feel helpless about how to address their children's health challenges.

As the owner of a boxing gym, I've noticed that many people wait until they have health issues before joining a gym and then try to stress themselves to diet and work out quickly to lose weight (especially at the beginning of the year). Just recently, I had a guy come to the boxing gym for a 1-on-1 personal training session, and he walked in the door eating fried chicken, French fries, and a biscuit in a box! I had to have a "real" conversation with him because showing up to a boxing gym with fast food in hand is a liability. What made his story stand out was after I asked him what his goal was for him to start boxing training, he told me he wanted to lose weight (smh). It's realities like this that I experience all the time. This is why I believe that it's important to educate younger generations about the importance of taking care of their health. A lot of adults have so many negative health concerns because what they were fed as kids became like a "blueprint" for how they should eat for life. I believe it's important for parents and school systems to prioritize feeding children nutritious foods to prevent future health issues and take proactive measures to avoid negative health outcomes.

The benefits of good health can inspire people to take their health seriously and challenge themselves to work towards their physical and mental potential. It is important to raise awareness about the negative outcomes of obesity, diabetes, physical pains, and medication needs (and costs). People should understand the real impact of these health issues before needing to make changes towards improving their health. Personally, I've witnessed the devastating effects of diabetes in my own family. Some of my family members had to undergo leg amputation and lose vision due to their addiction to sugary soda, snacks, and fast food. This experience was a wake-up call for me, and I hope more families won't have to face such realities before taking their health more seriously.

Parents and school systems should take a more proactive approach to educating younger generations about healthy food choices and being more mindful of their children's health. The only class where I received any information about food health was my physical education class in grade school. It introduced me to the food pyramid and discussed food groups, but that did not change my attitude about food. The most significant impact that shaped my awareness of food was boxing training. It wasn't until I took my first boxing class and had to do an hour and a half of workouts that I became the most tired I had ever been in my life. Even now, I can remember looking up at the end of the class while I was lying in the middle of the boxing ring and telling myself, "I am never going to feel like this ever again..."

After attending that first boxing class, I had an awakening and began to consider my food choices seriously. I realized that food directly impacts how the body responds to what you consume. Prior to boxing, I used to consume fast food, soda, alcohol, cannabis, and junk food. However, since taking boxing seriously, I haven't eaten fast food, drank soda, or indulged in potato chips in over two decades.

It's important for young people to understand the impact of their food choices on their health. Working out alone (or playing sports) isn't enough to protect a person's health. A person can't outwork a bad diet to become magically healthy. Looking back, I wish I had known more about how nutrition affects the body and mind before starting boxing. Now, I am making an effort to educate young people by scheduling a nutritionist to attend the boxing gym every semester and have conversations to educate families about healthier options. I also encourage people from the greater community to attend these seminars. In addition to the nutritionist visits, I constantly share my own health experiences and insights with my students to educate them about examples of what can happen to them when they eat well (or vice versa). I also discuss health topics from podcasts, books, and social media to encourage my students to prioritize their well-being.

To address the childhood obesity epidemic, parents need to lead by example and prioritize their own health. Parents prioritizing their health can also positively influence their children's health choices. This includes introducing and feeding children high-nutrient foods like fruits, whole grains, vegetables, and legumes. Parents must prioritize their health awareness and practice what they preach when educating their children.

We need to improve our mindset about food as a society. Rather than indulging in food for taste alone, we should emphasize the health benefits that food provides. Many people enjoy fast food, desserts, and sugary drinks for their taste, but these foods can cause terrible long-term damage that could outweigh any temporary enjoyment. As a progressive society, we must value food as a form of medicine for healing instead of just a source of pleasure.

Parents, schools, governments, and organizations should invest more in promoting a higher-nutrition lifestyle and prioritizing a healthier society. This proactive approach can improve individual health outcomes and reduce the collective burden of healthcare costs associated with poor nutrition. By sharing knowledge (and incentivizing eating better nutrition), we can reverse the trend of childhood obesity and improve the health of future generations.

Wellness Practices (e.g., working out or playing sports, knowledge of food choices, "What is food?")

It's important to incorporate wellness practices on a daily basis. Doing so establishes a healthy physical and mental habit and ensures that a person is working to improve themselves for their longevity. Examples of wellness practices include:

- Exercising - I recommend at least 20 minutes a day for five times a week.
- Eating high nutritious foods at every meal (and/or throughout the day).

- Prioritizing sleep – Recommended 6-8 hours straight nightly.
- Practicing self-awareness - Reflecting on how a person can improve their mindset and behaviors for 5-10 minutes at the end of each day.

Parents need to teach their child(ren) how to maintain wellness practices to better prepare them to succeed in school, extracurricular activities (e.g., sports or music), or any other situations. Whether creating routines for better eating habits or establishing a consistent workout schedule, wellness is something that EVERYBODY should prioritize.

There are various ways for people to practice wellness. Whether exercising by taking classes, participating in nutrition programs, or even fasting, practicing life-enhancing activities is a good thing. The most important factor is to establish a consistent schedule. It may be difficult to make the necessary tradeoffs to maintain consistency in wellness practices, as it requires sacrificing comfort and overcoming laziness. However, the benefits of improving both mind and body make these tradeoffs worthwhile. Committing to working out 5-6 times a week, going to bed earlier to wake up for morning workouts, and consuming more nutritious foods may not always be enjoyable, but they will ALWAYS be beneficial to an individual's overall well-being.

A person who wants to practice wellness needs to know WHY they want to do it personally. There will always be valid reasons why a person struggles to stay committed to a healthy routine. We can rationalize anything nowadays, and blaming others or making excuses are easy "outs" not to take accountability. We live in a world where we are more easily distracted than ever, and staying focused is a challenge that most people fail at all the time. It will take patience to fight towards achieving a certain level of wellness because temptations to not exercise when you said you were, get a quick bite of fast food between meals, or quit altogether and resort to old habits can be easy.

When parents set wellness goals for themselves (or their children), the key is to focus on long-term progress and dedication. To enhance wellness, it's helpful to prioritize different areas of focus, such as spiritual, physical, and emotional well-being. It's also important to set smaller achievable goals to make gradual progress. Creating a list of these goals and committing to a schedule for practicing them can help maintain focus and accountability. Whether it's through meditation, exercise, or eating healthier, are all fantastic priorities for self-improvement.

Aging

I feel like having conversations about aging is so important because it's such a natural transformation. There is so much to learn when it comes to the changes the body goes through as we get older. It is shocking to me that more people don't talk about the inevitable changes that happen to the brain and body as we age. Most people try to avoid discussing getting older out of fear of recognizing their own mortality. But these conversations don't have to be daunting. They can be positive, enlightening, and even comforting. This is ABSOLUTELY a subject that parents should discuss with their child(ren), and it should be done with a positive attitude. Most people, when they think about aging, are saddened. But the reality is that we all age more every day, and our bodies will naturally adapt through processes we can (and can't) control. I believe that if we as a society can honestly confront the realities of what happens when we age, we will be more prepared to understand what to expect and handle ourselves with more care.

We as a society should embrace aging because, as I like to say, "Getting old is the goal." Younger generations should be more educated about the natural changes of aging so that they will know how to adapt to their body changes (if they are fortunate enough to get older). This is something that we all have in common as human beings. A few common changes that take place when aging are menopause, erectile dysfunction, and eyesight weakening. As we age, it becomes harder to talk about aging-related changes we go through, partially because people are ashamed to explain the deterioration they're going through. It's important for adults to educate young people about these realities early on. This can help younger generations adapt to aging better and embrace the process.

Having discussions about aging with youth is fascinating because they can't fathom what it would be like to have physical decline. They are still testing their physical limits and assume that their energy will always be vibrant as long as they have food when they're hungry and rest when they get tired. The pains and scars they experience from playing or accidents always feel like they will recover quickly with time (or with the help of medicine). Modern-day medicine has allowed people to delay aging and be pain-free from taking pills and medications. For instance, taking certain supplements like glucosamine, chondroitin, or fish oil can reduce joint pain and improve mobility. Even understanding that their bladder will get smaller with aging, and they will have to go to the bathroom in the middle of the night to pee EVERY NIGHT! Also, learning that the body will become more potassium deficient when aging and will need to have foods on hand (like bananas or peanut butter) to eat quickly and stop cramps from happening throughout the day. Information like this is crucial for people to understand and be more prepared for what's to come when they get older. Information like this is helpful for youth to know before they experience aging so that they can understand that their body is going through a natural stage of development.

There should be an awareness of aging at much earlier ages (as early as elementary grades) to make it a common awareness throughout society. It is a real shock when you see your first grey hair, notice your skin starting to wrinkle a bit, or even when your bones start cracking more from wear and tear from losing cartilage. I've always wanted to know information before I experienced the "real thing," so I have always gravitated toward hanging around people older to learn from their experiences before I live my own. When it comes to aging, the WILDEST advice I've ever received when I asked an older gentleman, "What's it like to get older?" his answer was, "Just keep waking up in the morning, and you'll find out." I was like, "What type of advice is THAT??" and he just smiled and laughed.

It's even necessary that younger generations learn about aging because they will need to be responsible for their parents when they become elderly (and need to learn how to deal with those realities). Things like Alzheimer's, dementia, and the process of taking care of a loved one at home (or finding a good nursing home) should be common knowledge. By not discussing these topics (and acting like these things aren't going to happen), we lessen the scope of what could be done to improve the quality of life for so many people who will go through these processes.

I think that aging should be taught as a mandatory subject in grade school to discuss, prepare, and inform younger generations of the realities of getting older. The current way of learning about aging is to wait until problems and pains arise and then go see a doctor about a concern (to be handled privately). This reactive way of responding to concerns after something bad happens (or doesn't feel good) is shortsighted and fragile. Instead of being reactive after experiencing pain, we should become more proactive to improve our health to make aging better for our quality of life. Learning about the gradual stages of age-related changes in the body will make aging less scary. Awareness of aging shouldn't be an abyss of the unknown, but a common understanding of what changes will naturally occur within the body.

As a side note, I think formal (and informal) education around aging could foster more interest in advancements in the medical field. The intrigue of aging could help younger generations become more interested in nutrition and medicine, which could potentially influence people to become medical doctors for careers. Not only that, but society as a whole could benefit from having more amazing physical therapists, nurse practitioners, elderly caregivers, and other great administrators in the healthcare industry.

Aging is a natural process we all experience, and each of us goes through it differently. Understanding the changes that happen in our bodies can help us make better choices in life and educate younger generations to do the same. If parents prioritize their own well-being and self-care, they should not hesitate to talk to their children about aging. By prioritizing wellness and teaching young people to take care of themselves as they age, they can create a higher quality of life through wellness practices and age gracefully with less pain.

The 3rd Adulting Awareness: Life Skills

Life skills are essential to learning how to solve problems, live independently, and work well with others. Many life skills, like learning how to communicate with others, having manners, and being dependable, are responsibilities that start at home with parents. In preparing for these responsibilities, parents should help their child(ren) learn how to develop a work ethic and rely on their own capabilities (as they will need those skills to develop for their futures). As younger generations grow up, they will need to take over responsibilities that they will be hired to do (like working a job), become parents of their own children, or inherit an inheritance that they will be trusted to handle (and hopefully not squander it).

Developing life skills is important for both self-care and working with others to create a greater community. Youth should learn how to develop life skills by gaining work experience (domestically and for income), acquiring various skill sets (e.g., listening, communicating, etc.), and learning how to overcome mistakes. This can happen through participating in extracurricular activities (such as joining a sports team), taking responsibility for assigned domestic tasks at home (e.g., doing laundry, etc.), and working through having an internship or job.

Having a work ethic does not happen by accident. It takes wanting to fulfill desired outcomes and living up to higher standards to attain a certain goal. A person has to have high expectations to live up to and be incentivized to follow through with their mission. Parents should prioritize training their child(ren) to develop a work ethic because it is a form of developing independence. The lessons that younger generations should learn about having a work ethic is that it's needed to get tasks done and foster skills to be employed as an adult.

In modern times, many children are not being taught essential life skills such as doing laundry, managing social relationships, or fixing things around the house. Instead, parents often take on these responsibilities because they feel their child(ren) should focus solely on academics. However, the "real world" extends beyond school, and parents are not considering the long-term implications of not equipping their child(ren) with these fundamental skills. Passing standardized tests is important, as is learning how to cook and clean up after oneself. The work inside the classroom helps build careers, and the work outside of the classroom builds character. By learning to manage academic and domesticated tasks, younger generations can develop accountability, time management, and goal-setting skills that are essential for adulthood and leadership roles in their careers and relationships.

Work Ethics/Habits

Teaching work ethics to youth is important for preparing them for adulthood through increasing their abilities. This includes mastering a strong work ethic, learning to communicate effectively, networking, and practicing relationship-building skills. As younger generations work on developing these skills, they will inevitably face challenges that test their resolve. In order to endure adversity, they will need to develop confidence in self-efficacy and contribute to solving their own problems.

Developing work ethics for most people is not intrinsic. A person must want to get outside of their comfort zone to overcome their dissatisfaction with not achieving their potential (or goal). That level of self-awareness takes developing maturity to want to work towards achieving desired results and using their grit to motivate themselves into creating action. Oftentimes, it also comes from being around others (especially parents) who show what's possible from the results they earn. When people can see another's results, they can be influenced to want to have a drive because what they see is possible.

Children often live up to the standards set by the authority figures in their lives. Depending on their motivation, kids can be either enthusiastic and hardworking or unmotivated and lazy. At a moment's notice, they will adjust their effort level based on the expectations placed on them. As a boxing coach, I have found that I switch modes between acting as an "enforcer" or an "incentive guru" to motivate kids to perform. Being an "enforcer" involves being somewhat strict and implementing consequences to encourage lazy kids to become more focused. For instance, if I am teaching a student a new punch combination, I make sure to explain it in multiple ways and allow them to ask me questions and demonstrate it thoroughly. If I ask them to perform the new punch combination (and they forget), I tell them they need to face a consequence (like doing five pushups) to teach them to pay attention more. This is to have them practice being more of a critical thinker and retaining information better so that when they get older, they will be more reliable.

As an "incentive guru," the goal is to encourage children to work hard toward their goals. It is important to understand what motivates them and offer rewards that will incentivize their efforts. It's best to use incentives sporadically and thoughtfully to avoid creating an expectation of receiving rewards for every task. Punctuality, seeing tasks through to completion, and meeting deadlines are important skills for adulthood. Whether as an "enforcer" or "incentive guru," parents should use both methods to help their children develop better work ethics so that they are more prepared for adulthood.

I have a funny story about a time when I played the role of an "enforcer." One day when I was a teacher/coach at Emery Elementary, my students (who played for my basketball team) didn't turn in their homework on time. When I decided to do something to have them face a consequence, being an "enforcer" was to help them learn from their mistake. Let me explain...

One Friday afternoon, when I was teaching at Emery Elementary

School, I asked my all-boys class to pull out their math homework from the previous day and was totally shocked by what happened next. To my surprise, NONE of them did it! Not only was I disappointed, but I had spent the previous half-day going over the material and knew that they should have known how to do those assignments. But what infuriated me was that when I asked why they didn't do it, they said that they didn't know how to because they "forgot."

On that same day, later in the afternoon, we had our last regular season basketball game at home. I knew that the boys were looking forward to playing that basketball game in front of their families and friends, and decided to use that as motivation for them to do their assignments. Instead of trying to go back over the same material and teach it again, I made a decision. If they wanted to play in that basketball game, they needed to turn in their homework assignment by the end of the workday, or I would forfeit the game. I was determined to uphold accountability and responsibility. They did NOT like that, but I stood my ground. They had taken my teaching time for granted, and I was not going to let that slide. They would have to figure out what I had already taught them the previous day, or I would forfeit the game.

Suddenly, they started to huddle and collaborate by putting their desks together to talk amongst themselves and to try to follow the directions in the textbook together. They were scrambling and yelling at each other to figure out how to solve the problems. When they tried to ask me questions to try and give them the answers, I politely told them, "I went over everything yesterday for two hours and asked you if you had any questions then, and you told me "No." Now, you must figure out how to do what you saw me do yesterday when I reviewed the answers."

At 2:45 pm, the visiting team pulled up and was escorted to the changing room. By this time, the neighborhood families and friends had started to arrive for our scheduled home game (which was supposed to start at 3:30 pm). Little did anyone outside of that classroom know that my team wasn't even getting ready to perform in the last game of the season. Instead, my students were panicking from stressing over losing time from not paying attention the day before and knew that I was seriously about to end their season in the classroom instead of on the court.

When it reached 3 o'clock, and the students had not finished the assignments on time, I hit the buzzard to notify the principal's office. As the sounds of smacking lips and yelling statements like "Oh my God!" were made, I waited for the answer from the front office to pick up. When our wonderful school secretary (Mrs. Hall) picked up the call, I told her, "Mrs. Hall, I have a situation. My boys didn't do their homework last night, which I thoroughly went over yesterday during class, and because they didn't do what I asked them to do, I am going to forfeit our home game. I will come down and greet the opposing team and coaches and let them know in a few minutes. Please make an announcement that we won't be playing our home game today. Thank you."

To Ms. Hall's surprise, she was shocked by the decision but supported my reasoning for what I decided to do and told me, "OK, Mr. Brown, no problem, I'll let everyone know." When I went down to the gym, it was PACKED with people. Parents, families, and friends from both teams were present, and everything was already set up with the music playing. I walked right up to the head coach and his staff and told him that we were going to forfeit the game and why. He called his team over to us and asked them to take a knee. He told them in front of me that he admired what I was doing, and that it took courage for me to make the decision to forfeit the game to put academics over athletics. He reminded his team that they were first STUDENT-athletes and that being a student came before being an athlete. As word spread around town that I decided to forfeit the basketball game because my students didn't do their schoolwork, word spread around town, and people started to refer to me as "Coach Carter" (a reference to the movie about a basketball coach who faced adversity with his basketball team). My students will never forget my example of forfeiting that basketball game that day. I hope that they are grown men with integrity and character now and that I have a small part to play in helping them with setting priorities through my example.

That day, I taught my students that life has consequences when you don't do the right things, and it's always better to do what's right (whether it's convenient for you or not). My decision to forfeit the basketball game was to help them realize that when you don't do what you're responsible for, you should face some sort of consequences. I think this type of thinking is beneficial for helping raise the next generation. I do not think it helps people mature when they get away with not doing what they are supposed to do or that earning grades and awards should just be given (side note: I'm not a fan of "participation trophies"). It is a privilege to play sports on a team, and as their coach, I was using my leverage to prioritize their education over their athletics.

As adults, we must model what we want younger generations to see as good leadership. We also must help them learn to evolve in creating morals and positive judgment to enhance their own decision-making abilities. Even though my students didn't like my decision to forfeit the game at the time, I hope they later realized that I was worthy of respect and that I was just doing what was academically beneficial for them (which I thought was important). The lesson that I wanted my students to learn was that it wasn't just about turning in a homework assignment but that I was preparing them for the expectations they would have in the "real world."

Encouraging young people to develop a strong work ethic is crucial for their professional and personal relationships.

Children learn their standards from their parents and authority figures, so setting a good example is important for their potential. In addition to developing a strong work ethic, younger generations need to learn life skills like effective communication, networking, and building relationships. These are some life skills that parents can help their kids learn crucial attributes to attaining success in their adulthood.

Communicating

Communicating is an important skill to teach younger generations to respect because it impacts every aspect of their lives (including their "self-talk"). From finding the best employment opportunities to befriending people in convenient places, communicating has multiple benefits. Learning to communicate effectively also helps with creating solutions to conflict resolution and public speaking when engaging with audiences. Communicating is an important ability to connect with others, which is inseparable from success in adulthood.

Parents need to take a more proactive approach to help their children communicate better because learning how to socialize displays maturity and builds a good reputation. To achieve this, parents should help their child(ren) practice initiating conversations and become comfortable with the discomfort of interacting with strangers. Learning to take the "risk" of initiating conversations can lead to increased confidence, improved communication, and a respectful attitude towards meeting new people.

Since many parents have given their child(ren) tablets and cell phones since they were infants, younger generations are often more reserved and can be more socially awkward than generations of the past. Part of the reason is that ever since kids were younger, children were handed a device to occupy their time whenever they had any "downtime" (or when parents wanted to keep their child(ren) busy). As younger generations grew older, they didn't learn to observe the world around them and pick up on nonverbal and verbal communication skills. Instead of learning how to make small talk by being around others (and showing interest in them), younger generations kept their heads down, looking at screens that were more convenient and fun to watch. The lack of practice of learning how to socialize with others wasn't honed, and as they grow up, they find it socially awkward to engage with others in person (especially those they aren't familiar with in public spaces).

Even in situations where it would be socially respectful to speak and acknowledge someone conveniently (e.g., walking into someone's home, meeting for an interview, etc.), younger generations often lack the confidence to speak to people publicly (especially speaking to others first). To improve communication skills, it's important to take the "risk" of initiating conversations and asking questions to get to know others. Being able to speak to others shows confidence and also lets others know that a person is friendly. Becoming more comfortable speaking with others starts with paying attention to others in the same space and observing what might make people around them interesting to talk to. Acknowledging something that a person may find interesting about others (and expressing their admiration) shows a level of respect, which makes environments feel safer because of the civility shown. These skills need to be taught to younger generations so that when they mature into spaces as adults, they will have the know-how and be comfortable engaging with others.

I am ALWAYS coaching my students to get better at communicating with EVERYBODY who visits my boxing gym.

I do so by helping them speak up, introduce themselves, and practice speaking to each other (and guests) every day. Being able to communicate with others is a skill that takes practice to become comfortable doing. To help my students (and clients) be more comfortable speaking to people at the boxing gym, I use a formula to ensure that people feel seen and respected in every engagement. The formula is simple and helps people to smile and reciprocate a positive mindset as they visit:

- Give a nice greeting with a smile and introduce yourself. I teach my students (and clients) to greet others with respect and the energy they would like to feel in return. I try to get my students to greet others by not being too judgmental and negative in their approach. Being willing to speak first with a smile can lower anxieties and make a person entering the boxing gym and feel safe. This creates an immediate positive environment that lowers people's guard while also making them feel like a "celebrity." The moment they recognize that others value them, they want to respond by paying the respect back with kindness. That first smiling engagement and asking, "How are you feeling?" goes a long way toward making others enjoy their time and makes people feel better that they came.

- Offer a compliment about something specific that you notice about them. I tell my students (and clients) to notice something they might admire about someone's appearance and say something nice. Whether they admire their fashion, hairstyle, or whatever may stand out to them, make a statement to make them feel more confident about being themselves.

- Ask a follow-up question to learn what they might have in common. Some examples can be, "Did you watch the game last night or sports?" or "Have you learned anything you think is worthy of sharing?" These "soft" questions create "small talk" that helps people learn more about each other.

- Reciprocate and share something you learned that day with them, too. Others typically want to open up after you're willing to listen to them first. *Work on learning from others and try to stay vibrant throughout the course of the conversation.

An honest and truthful approach is essential for effective communication. It involves having integrity, showing respect, and being a good listener. The best communicators I know are honest, respectful, and slow to anger. They seek the truth, avoid pettiness, and refrain from making negative judgments without knowing all the facts. It's important for parents to teach their child(ren) to communicate with others in a respectful manner, just as they would like to be treated. Parents can provide opportunities for their child(ren) to improve their child's (ren's) communication skills by encouraging them to introduce themselves in new environments or placing orders (e.g., ordering their meal at a restaurant, etc.). These kinds of opportunities help younger generations practice having the confidence to speak up for themselves (which helps them gain independence). This is all practice to help them have better social interactions to help them have a higher quality of life. When people learn to have great engagement with others, they can help put themselves in better relationships to advance in all kinds of potential positive outcomes.

Networking

Networking is a very important skill to teach younger generations to master because it's how they learn about the developments happening around them. Parents should explain to their child(ren) that networking is how you find out about jobs, meet people who have businesses that you could benefit from, and broaden your knowledge beyond your current circumstances. At its core, networking is finding commonality with someone you don't know (initially) and seeing if you become friendly enough to create a mutual benefit.

Networking is a skill that involves communicating with new people to meet a need. Sometimes, it's not even about swapping resources but just making great relationships for friendship. Parents should teach their kids about the value of networking because initiating relationships with good people creates opportunities for personal advancement. I LOVE networking because people have all types of interesting resources that I would find interesting. Even if I felt like I had met a person who would be a good resource to someone else I know, I wouldn't hesitate to offer to make an introduction. Networking provides surprises that can benefit everyone when people are willing to share opportunities where it makes sense.

There are multiple ways to find networking opportunities. Conventional places where people meet to network are social parties, sporting events, bars, golfing, conferences, and other social settings. There are many other pursuits to foster networking opportunities. Some other options are buying memberships and joining private clubs to do interesting things where you can meet new people with like-minded interests.

Networking should be taught as a valuable life skill. Parents should encourage their children to become more comfortable speaking up to meet others (e.g., networking). There are many opportunities for personal growth through social connections, which might also lead to financial gain. While at home, parents should start educating their child(ren) on the importance of how to interact with others in public spaces. Most times, when opportunities arise, there is only ONE chance to make a good impression. Communicating effectively while networking can create new opportunities when those slim-chance encounters are done correctly.

While growing up, parents (and other authority figures) often tell their child(ren), "Don't talk to strangers!" But when you grow up and become an adult, you must learn to talk to strangers ALL THE TIME! Parents should teach their child(ren) HOW to talk to strangers because learning how to do so can create many great opportunities in their child's future. When younger generations grow up and become employed, they will need to talk to strangers to engage with new clients, communicate with customers, respond to inquiries, and more. I tend to believe that talking to strangers is one of the best ways to enhance your personal value because you can meet new people and broaden your horizons. The more people you meet, the higher chances you have to make friends who can share their network, which leads to more access to options to gain more resources.

Networking is not a natural human instinct. It's a skill that younger generations need to be taught and nurtured. As parents, you play a crucial role in this. When your child(ren) sees you taking an interest in and valuing certain behaviors, they should understand why you're impressed and are encouraged to learn those same traits. Children are impressionable, and what they see is what they will mimic. Therefore, it's important for parents to model respectful and effective communication as an example of how their child(ren) should interact with others.

Parents need not only to demonstrate effective communication and networking skills but also to incentivize their child(ren) to practice the desired behavior themselves. Whether it's giving more permission to do something desirable their child would like to do (e.g., play video games, watch movies, etc.) or a simple praise of acknowledgment to congratulate their child's attempt to do a good job speaking up. Parents should reward their child's effort to learn new skills.

Lastly, parents should take their child(ren) on outings to places where they can practice communicating and networking together. Certain days of the week can be prioritized as "Communication Day" or "Networking Day" to help their child(ren) challenge themselves to speak first to others in an effort to make a connection. The goal is to challenge younger generations to network on a "Communication Day" or "Networking Day." Whether they choose to speak to someone they don't know by greeting them first or taking the initiative to prioritize doing something nice to help make someone's day better. These are practice attempts to get younger generations to learn how to become better communicators and network well. When parents take time to educate and practice with their kids the skills of communicating and networking with others, they can become more prepared to handle networking with more confidence as adults in their futures.

Relationships

In my opinion, having good relationships is one of the most important factors in life. The type of relationships that a person cultivates can impact their mental health, networking opportunities, and overall well-being. As parents, you have the opportunity to help your child(ren) learn how to build relationships. These relationships are important not just for their personal lives but also for their future professional success.

I personally try to build relationships wherever I go. I try to talk to people at grocery stores, restaurants, and everywhere where I can. Taking the chance to volunteer a compliment, offer help to someone in need, or speak to greet others are good opportunities to start relationships. You NEVER know who someone is upon first meeting them, so being respectful and civil is always preferred.

When people think about starting most relationships, they often consider what they can get from it first. Most people are concerned about their own needs and wants and are constantly worried (or concerned) about their own self-preservation. But I've learned that the best relationships are based on service to each other. If you've ever been fortunate enough to talk to married couples that have been in their relationships for decades, they will tell you that endless forgiveness and serving each other are what makes their relationships last. It's not realistic to approach every relationship with that mentality, but we can all learn from that way of thinking.

I think the value of teaching younger generations about creating relationships should be taught like any mandatory subject in grade school (e.g., math, reading, etc.). As adults, we know how important good relationships are, but we often fail to teach younger generations the importance of actively cultivating them with the right intentions. Interactions in business, romantic partnerships, and other relationships would all be better if people learned how to conversate better. Instead of assuming that younger generations will naturally learn this, parents must consciously teach their child(ren) the significance of building (and maintaining) healthy relationships. Getting good at relationships will not happen through passive circumstances but through being proactive toward building positive engagements. Therefore, parents should be proactive about communicating to their child(ren) that relationship-building is essential for their future well-being.

There are also times when younger generations will encounter people who aren't the type of people they would like to communicate with. In situations like that, they will still need to figure out how to get along with others with civility. Sometimes, customers, clients, bosses, and others can be uneasy to get along with (and draining to be around). Dealing with challenging customers, clients, bosses, and others is inevitable. Showing patience and being mature enough to handle those interactions positively (without panicking) helps keep a person's sanity and is an important skill to develop. Whether it's work-related or a personal relationship, being mature and not reverting to a nasty attitude shows character and professionalism. This understanding needs to be discussed with younger generations so that when they get into the "real world," they can know how to control their emotions and work towards creating solutions.

Regardless of race, economic class, or social status, we can all agree that forming connections is crucial in adulthood. Assisting younger generations with learning communication skills (whether introverted or extroverted) can help them navigate public life and other relationships they will encounter. No one can fulfill all their needs alone, so forming relationships is crucial for personal and professional growth. Actively listening to others, initiating conversations, and addressing conflicts are all effective ways to be a positive presence in relationships. As adults, it's important for us to continually prepare younger generations to excel at building relationships, as this will aid in their independence as they enter adulthood.

Current Events

Staying abreast of what's happening in the world is essential and becoming more difficult by the day. Everything in life feels like it's moving faster and faster. Trying to learn the latest trends in technology, local and national news, and finances feels more urgent to our daily survival. With all of the platforms available to learn about current events (e.g., Instagram, Facebook, TikTok, etc.), parents should constantly communicate with their kids about what they're consuming online.

As a society, we are getting our news through various resources that are not always centered around shared truths. The way we access information has changed dramatically in our lifetime. It has become more varied and complex. From cable news to social media platforms, the speed of receiving information has increased, and it has become more difficult to discern what is true due to misinformation.

As consumers of news outlets, we need to be more diligent about what we give our attention to. It's now our responsibility as viewers to fact-check, research the background of reporting sources, and take other individual initiatives. Unfortunately, we can no longer assume that what's shown on a screen (or what we read) is shared truth for our collective goodwill. Therefore, we must seek out multiple sources of information to uncover the most reliable truth.

When parents want to help their child(ren) understand the importance of staying informed, they must explain to their child(ren) why what's happening in the world can affect them. When I talk to kids about current events, it feels like there are two different realities between what they're seeing, and what adults are seeing. Kids are usually fixated on what's relevant amongst their peers, while their parents are politically frustrated and busy trying to "keep their head above water." Younger generation's awareness is centered around what's the most viral video circulating (which usually includes the latest TikTok dance and other entertainment), but also what algorithms suggest to them based on what content has caught their attention previously. So, the content youth will be provided will not often be what their parents will be exposed to. While parents are often still watching conventional news (e.g., CNN, Fox News, Facebook, etc.) to get their news sources, they don't have the time to seek out newness through having ample spare time. Oftentimes, there is no overlap of shared information that parents and their kids are seeing through their information platforms at the same time. Some things that younger generations are consuming do not remotely have the same awareness some adults have (and vice versa). So, if parents want to make more of an effort to bring their kids' awareness into learning the benefits of current events, they need to spend time advising their kids about why learning "adulting" news is relevant to them. It's also important for parents to ask their kids questions about what they're learning so that they can become familiar with how their kids are thinking and learning themselves.

Learning about current events benefits younger generations by informing them about general topics that the public should be aware of. Part of a parent's job is raising their kid's awareness of issues that will affect their future options. When younger generations are informed about things that concern them, they can make proactive adjustments to improve their future circumstances.

Sports

Sports can teach discipline, teamwork, and problem-solving skills. They also provide opportunities to learn how to handle both success and failure (which is crucial for success in adulthood). Parents should consider enrolling their child(ren) in sports for several reasons. Sports offer a great to build relationships with others who share similar interests, learn to collaborate with teammates to achieve common goals, and develop greater self-awareness.

I strongly believe that every child should participate in team sports to learn how to lead and follow others, and should also engage in individual sports to learn self-mastery. Both aspects emphasize personal growth and developing a mindset to enhance personal responsibility. Engaging in both types of sports helps develop tools to deal with stressful situations, regulate emotional maturity, and cope with uncertainty. Sports are like internships for learning about the "real world". The skills practiced in organized sports create lifelong memories that can be used to build bonds, friendships, and learn how to process winning (or losing). These experiences help develop character and grit, and the memories can be shared to inspire others later in life. Every parent should invest in getting their child(ren) involved in sports, as the benefits of these experiences compound into a lifetime of wisdom.

Parents should encourage their child(ren) to get into sports (even if they don't "like" sports). Engaging in sports activities helps younger generations to develop their skill sets and face challenges (which in turn can help them build qualities such as patience and discipline). When parents want to introduce sports to their child(ren), they should discuss with their child(ren) why they think a certain kind of sport would be a good idea for them to participate in. Then, they should expose their child(ren) to the sport to gauge their interest. Kids oftentimes are exposed to a sport by watching people play on television, in physical education class in school, or learning about what sports their friends are interested in.

In many scenarios, a kid's environment dictates their interest based on what they're exposed to. For instance, sports involving balls (such as basketball, football, soccer, etc.) are more commonly found in inner cities, while sports requiring sticks (like hockey, tennis, polo, etc.) are prevalent in suburban communities. Additionally, the association of certain countries with specific sports (e.g., Canada with hockey, the United States with football, Brazil with soccer, etc.) can also impact cultural interest in a sport. A common thread to getting exposed to sports is having access to resources and being introduced through association.

If a child shows interest in a sport, parents can enroll them in a class, have them try out for a team, or buy personal training sessions to let them try it out. It's important to introduce sports to kids by letting them play them, watch professional and amateur-level games, and explaining the potential benefits (e.g., college scholarships, professional careers, etc.). Regardless of what sport a child chooses, prioritizing getting kids into sports is essential for their health, intellect, and social maturity.

Lastly, sports play a crucial role in teaching young people how to become leaders within a hierarchical system. By following instructions from coaches, they learn to take advice as they would from a boss. They also learn to become patient while working with others, and understand the significance of their roles within a team. Engaging in sports also helps younger generations discover more about themselves and realize the importance of practice for improvement. Parents should ensure that their child(ren) participates in sports not only for physical and mental well-being, but also to learn valuable life lessons from being part of a team (or individual sports). The benefits of sports are endless, and practicing these skills can be very useful in adulthood.

Learning how to L.E.A.R.N.

Younger generations need to learn many things to become proficient at "adulting." Earning (and managing) finances, taking care of one's body, and communicating effectively with others are just a few examples that come to mind. As essential as these factors are as adults, many people don't have role models to teach them these vital skills and typically have to figure these skills out on their own. No matter what background a person is from, whether they grew up in the city, suburbs, or rural areas, having great communication skills can help a person become successful.

While many of these skills are acquired over time, they are not always taught in schools or by parents (leaving individuals to figure them out on their own). It would have been beneficial for many of us to learn these awarenesses as youth growing up, and now we have an opportunity to help prevent younger generations from facing unnecessary challenges. One of the best skills that adults can do to help younger generations prepare for adulthood is to improve their communication skills. To help young people learn how to become more prepared for adulthood, I created an acronym, "L.E.A.R.N.," to help with bettering communication abilities. The acronym L.E.A.R.N. stands for: Listen, Emphasize, Articulate, Retain, and Negotiate.

L.E.A.R.N. is designed to provide tips to help younger generations improve their communication skills so that when they become adults, they can navigate situations independently. As adults, we engage in various types of relationships (e.g., work, family, kids, etc.) and need to communicate effectively at the core of all these relationships. By learning how to L.E.A.R.N., younger generations (and their parents) can enhance their communication skills and better handle the challenges of interacting with diverse personalities and characters in the future.

Listed below are what "L.E.A.R.N." means in terms and definitions:

L – Listen – Listening to learn.
E – Emphasize – Become respectfully energized to get your point across.
A – Articulate – Help people visually understand where you're coming from (like an artist).
R - Retain – Retrain your brain to memorize information.
N – Negotiate – Work things out through patience and common ground.

Besides the terms and definitions, below are breakdowns of how to apply each term (in detail). As a boxing coach, I use these to communicate more effectively with others, and they have helped me connect with countless people throughout my interactions.

L – Listen – Listening to learn

Younger generations should be taught that listening to learn from others benefits both themselves and the person they're listening to. Listening is a valuable skill that allows the listener to gain knowledge from another person's perspective. It also expands their own thinking and creates connections with others. It takes maturity to listen. A person must want to submit when someone else wants to speak, be engaging while showing respect, and be selfless in sharing their time. The act of listening gives permission to put others first and seek to understand how they think. In the process, a person should want to have the mindset to learn from what is being shared and retain what's being relayed.

Since childhood, we have been trained only to listen when it benefits us in some way. As children, being called by our names made a lot of us feel like we were about to get in trouble, about to get a reward, or that someone needed something from us. Speaking from a male's perspective, males are often raised to value listening when we are called to solve an emergency or when someone needs our help. When our names are called, we rush into thinking about what we need to do quickly to solve a problem or give a response to move on to our next task. As I've grown older, I have learned not to be so defensive when listening and not just listen to ONLY solve problems. Now, I focus on listening to be present and allow whoever I'm speaking with to feel respected by prioritizing their perspectives. Sometimes, it's important to let someone vent to say what they're thinking out loud and be patient with them, like how I would want them to be to me (if I were in their "shoes"). In cases like that, it's best to just observe and listen without judgment.

Younger generations need to understand that there is a difference between hearing and listening to things. A person can hear something from across the street (or even a person talking to them), but a person must concentrate on listening to be able to comprehend what is happening (or focus on what another person is saying). Listening involves deep concentration and a willingness to be mentally vulnerable to receiving information. When people listen to what others have to say, they can retain new information by understanding details and allowing others to feel dignified by sharing their perspectives.

To become a better listener, a person should slow down their thoughts to quiet their mind, just to listen to learn what others are saying. Too often, most people are thinking about their response to what someone is saying to them (while the person is still talking) and want to give a quick answer to appear "sharp" after they finish talking. Instead, it's more valuable to be fully present, openly listen to what others are trying to communicate, and then respond after hearing all of what a person has to say. When a person can slow down their urge to interject their opinion, it allows a person to fully understand what information is being presented to them. I try to teach my students at the boxing gym to "Actively Listen" while others are speaking to them. The practice of "Actively Listening" is paying attention until someone is finished speaking and then responding afterward to give feedback. Waiting until someone has completed their statement is important because the most interesting point they're trying to make is usually at the end of what they have to say.

For those parents who want to help their child(ren) learn how to listen better, there are ways to practice "Active Listening" that I would recommend. In the boxing gym, I practice teaching my students different ways to listen and retain information, which I call "The 6 Steps of Listening." I even practice using these steps in my daily life, and they always help me retain information during conversations. These steps can help younger generations practice giving their undivided attention and become better retainers of information in conversation.

"The 6 Steps of Listening" are as follows:

(1) Stop or pause what you're doing. *If you have any devices in your hands, put them to the side or put them away to concentrate better.
(2) Turn to face the person speaking to you. *Also, practice

making eye contact when listening and try not to move around a lot to concentrate more.

(3) Desire to retain what is being said and try to refrain from interrupting someone before they finish talking.

(4) Listen closely until everything a person has to say has been spoken. *Typically, the most important information is at the end of what somebody wants to say.

(5) Be able to learn from (and repeat) what was said to have made your time valuable from the conversation.

(6) If you didn't understand what someone was trying to tell you at first, don't hesitate to ask them a question to clarify your understanding. *It shows others that you care about what they were trying to share with you.

When "Actively Listen" to others, it can help them feel respected and valued. By practicing "Active listening," individuals can improve their relationships in various aspects of their lives (such as work, family, and personal interactions). Developing good communication skills (especially "Active Listening") can help younger generations cultivate qualities like patience, maturity, and respect for others. When young people communicate effectively, it not only benefits their well-being but also positively impacts everyone around them. In addition to working hard and achieving good academic results, it's important for younger generations to invest in improving their listening skills, as their future success depends on it.

E – Emphasize – Become respectfully energized to get your point across.

Learning how to emphasize a clear thought, argument, or opinion helps others want to learn from a person's perspective.

When a person is good at emphasizing their own point of view, they come across as confident, outspoken, and charismatic. On the other hand, those who struggle with emphasizing their points often feel misunderstood, disrespected, and insecure. To become better at emphasizing their points, people must think in terms of how they're being "received" by others and imagine what they are experiencing while listening to them.

Whenever a person speaks, they have a responsibility for every word spoken (and mostly the way it is received). Often, to be effective in communicating with others, a person must imagine how what they are saying will resonate with those they are speaking with. As a person who is speaking with others, it's almost like a person must step back and see themselves in the third person. That takes "getting outside of yourself" and viewing you like how a student would listen to a teacher. For instance, if you were in the position of listening to yourself speak, imagine what the experience would be like listening to you from someone else's point of view. How would you like to listen to YOU? Would you enjoy it? Would you feel more energized (or depleted) after being around you? Whatever you can imagine, you have some influence over how you communicate with others (and how they feel when spending time with you). People must resist the thought that everyone they speak with is as smart as they are, has the same sense of humor, and not assume others are just like themselves. Speaking with others is partly to educate or inform. Taking the time to emphasize points well helps others become better by listening to a person.

Emphasizing when it comes to communicating with others means being able to speak with excitement to avoid being hard to understand. This means teaching youth to speak with grace and empathy while also being excited about what they have to say. That comes down to having a positive attitude and using one's personality to be interesting. Some tips to emphasize a person's delivery in conversation are to speak with conviction, be excited about what they're talking about, and use body language to convey more meaning. When a person speaks with conviction by emphasizing their points while dialoguing with others, they are effectively using their voice not to be boring and avoid misunderstandings.

It's important for parents to remember that they are raising their kids to become independent adults. Teaching youth how to communicate effectively will help them succeed in all their future relationships (whether it's at work, in marriage, or in public interactions). As responsible adults, our main duty should be to prepare the next generation for independent living so they can take care of themselves and handle their future responsibilities.

A – Articulate – Help people visually understand where you're coming from (like an artist).

When communicating with others, a person has a responsibility to take charge of what they say (and how they say it). Articulating involves speaking clearly to communicate how a person wants to relay a message, offer help, or ask a question to get clarification about something. When a person can articulate well, it shows maturity, good manners, and a degree of self-awareness. Whether at work, placing an order, or having a general conversation, articulating well is good for being understood (which is essential for communicating effectively).

Younger generations should learn to articulate well for their professional and personal well-being. Whether it's making a first impression for a job interview, asking someone out for a first date, or communicating with others in daily life, articulation is a crucial skill that everyone should strive to improve on. Parents should value instilling articulation practice in their child(ren) as early as possible so that their child(ren) can be proficient in communicating with others throughout their lives. Younger generations should be taught to practice working to improve their communication abilities (specifically articulation) because they will create a good or bad reputation for themselves by how they communicate. People don't think about this much, but if a person comes off as not having good articulation (and not speaking clearly), others will find it difficult to have conversations with them and will want to distance themselves from feeling frustrated.

There are a variety of factors that contribute to how a person articulates. It starts at home with how parents speak to their child(ren) and how they express their behavior. Language like accents and cultural sayings start to be repeated, and a person's environment becomes a behavioral and articulate standard. It gets readjusted when kids start going to school and interacting with other kids. Interactions with peers start to influence a child's articulation, and they start to repeat other words and slang that they pick up on. Besides parent's influence on their child's (ren's) articulation, educational environments, and social circle "norms" become huge influences on how a person articulates. As younger generations get older, they will need to improve their articulation to problem solve, improve conflict resolution, and decrease misunderstandings.

The ability to articulate is essential. When parents teach their child(ren) that speaking clearly helps them get their needs understood, it encourages kids to be more proactive in speaking up for themselves. As humans, we constantly need to communicate our needs and wants, so being able to articulate helps with our own survival. If adults want to help younger generations mature and become successful adults, it's important to educate younger generations to communicate effectively by prioritizing the skill of articulation.

R - Retain – Retrain your brain to memorize information.

Learning to retain information is crucial for managing many aspects of our lives. It involves everything from remembering important dates, such as anniversaries and birthdays, to our academic lessons (e.g., tests, homework) and important work tasks (e.g., deadlines, assignments, etc.). The value of learning to retain information is immense and is the most important factor in improving a person's intelligence. Most of our lives are based on learning information. Being able to receive information, retain what was said, and act correctly based on what was learned shows that a person is capable of handling responsibilities. Demonstrating the ability to retain information shows maturity. When people can retain what they are paying attention to, they're adding value to their self-worth.

By training young people to retain information in schools (and at home), we can prepare them for the responsibilities they will have in the future. When parents prioritize helping their kids practice retaining information, they are instilling a lifelong discipline that will benefit them for years to come. Younger generations need to learn the importance of retaining information because it will help them become more employable, better partners and parents, and better contributors to society as a whole. Prioritizing retaining information as a skill should always be intentionally practiced, increasing the "IQ" of younger generations toward their future success.

There are many ways people can practice retaining information. Some ways are telling (and listening) to stories, doing rote work, or playing games. Others are taking notes, recording audio, or watching videos. Regardless of what method works best for each individual, we can all benefit from having more options for learning how to retain new things. In the boxing gym, I make it a priority that EVERYONE who comes to train with me will learn something every day. My goal is that no matter how someone comes into the gym, by the time they leave, they have become a better person based on what they learned from being there.

To help my students retain information, I review what they learned from their time in the boxing gym at the end of each class (or personal training session). For instance, right after practice, I ask them "Tell me 2 things that you learned before you go?" This makes them think about what they learned by pausing and reflecting on what they've experienced. If they remember two or more things, I will reward them by getting excited and telling them, "I'm SO proud of YOU! You learned something new today! Great Job!" If they can't remember 2-3 things clearly, I drop hints of what I went over (e.g., "What's two combinations we went over today?" or "What's one of the latest current events we talked about today?"). If they STILL don't remember, I will become an "enforcer" and penalize them for forgetting what we went over (e.g., "Do 10 pushups for not remembering what we talked about earlier today.").

I do this not just to reprimand them for not paying attention but also for not valuing their time (and mine). It also sets a standard that the next time they come to the boxing gym, they should pay more attention to what is being discussed. What I'm doing is preparing younger generations for what is to be expected of them in the "real world." If they aren't paying attention to someone breaking down skills for them clearly, asking if they understand what they learned (and they agree), and they STILL can't remember at the end of a 1-hour session, to me, that's a problem. I think about what will happen as they are responsible for life tasks outside of the boxing gym (with more serious consequences). Things like being behind the wheel of an automobile or working a job in the future. We need younger generations to be capable of retaining information (and executing it) to entrust them with more serious responsibilities. The boxing gym is like a training ground for the "real world." What I'm trying to help my students prioritize is that retaining information is important, and they should be more focused and held accountable for their actions. I'm also trying to get them to value their time, appreciate learning new things, and not squander opportunities.

More tips to help younger generations learn to retain information:

- Make rote work important for them to practice. Have them write down information over and over (e.g., writing a quote 50 times on paper, etc.). Doing this helps a person remember information through repetition. This is a "throwback" approach to recalling information, but it works with spelling words, math, remembering quotes, language, and more.
- Incentivize - People get motivated by what they want (e.g., prizes, permissions, etc.). Telling a person they can get "X" after they do "X" helps them be goal-driven and motivated.
- Penalize – Most people are risk-averse and don't like losing something they already have. Facing a penalty (e.g., taking away a cell phone, less video game time, etc.) is a different kind of motivation.
- Better training—Private tutoring or one-on-one coaching can help reduce distractions and increase time spent on a subject or skill.

N – Negotiate – Work things out through patience and common ground

As a parent, you want your child(ren) to grow up and become a successful adult. Part of this journey will involve them leaving their comfort zones and experiencing the "real world." As they grow up, they will need to interact with others to work out compromises and solve differences. Some of these situations will involve making compromises and negotiating to settle disagreements. Negotiation is an important skill as a person gets older because it's unavoidable that a person is going to have conflict in their lives. As human beings, we are always jockeying for a position with others (we can't help ourselves). We want others to live life like we do and abide by the same standards and values that we have. Since that's unlikely to happen most of the time, we need to learn how to negotiate and be civil when sharing the same environment. Therefore, learning negotiating skills will help younger generations learn to handle challenging disputes and seek to be competitive to fight for their self-worth.

Negotiations are a part of business dealings when entering contracts. As younger generations want to buy "big ticket" items (e.g., homes, cars, etc.), they should prioritize negotiating for better pricing. In some situations, unjust dealings happen where some people "jack up the price" and try to take advantage of others. In cases like that, a person must speak up for their position to negotiate a "fairer" opportunity for themselves. When younger generations want to learn how to negotiate, they must understand the importance of comparing rates and determining the value of something. Being able to present comparable research to negotiate a fair cost can influence the seller or overseer to make a concession. It is important for parents to instill in their child(ren) a mindset of applying negotiation tactics (to resolve conflicts) and achieve favorable outcomes.

When the COVID-19 pandemic started in 2019, my boxing gym closed in March 2020 because businesses had to shut down due to mandated restrictions. Despite the shutdown restrictions, the landlord who owns the space that I lease for my boxing gym, had demanded that I still pay my lease on time every month. I didn't feel like that was fair, so I negotiated a deal with them to NOT pay the lease as long as the lockdowns were in effect. Instead, we worked out a deal that extended the lease for the duration of the lockdown restrictions. The lockdowns lasted for three months, so we agreed to write up a new contract to amend my lease for another three months. That way, the owners of the property didn't lose any money, and I didn't have to pay when I wasn't making money (because it was illegal for the business to be open). My point in sharing this story is to give insight into why negotiations matter when it comes to handling situations in "adulting." A person can't predict when they are going to hit unexpected difficulties, and learning how to adjust to demands through negotiating better terms is essential. Sharing stories like this is a great example to share with younger generations to help them potentially save their businesses or understand that learning to negotiate can save their livelihood.

The skill of negotiating is applicable to many different aspects of life. Whether asking someone out on a date or asking for a raise or promotion, learning to negotiate is a necessary skill in many life situations. Parents can offer tips to help teach their child(ren) learn how to be better when negotiating, by sharing and expressing their stories of engaging in challenging circumstances themselves (and telling the results). Another way of practicing negotiating skills is learning how to compare the cost of goods and services. Practices like doing research to compare prices, can influence a seller of goods or services to offer better prices. Showing evidence of another business offering the same good or service at a lower price can make for more favorable terms for the buyer. In other situations, character traits like asking nicely or offering to buy more in bulk (to pay a lower cost for each) can be enticing enough for a seller of goods to negotiate a better deal.

For example, when I first started my boxing gym, I KNEW I would have to spend a lot of money on buying equipment to fill up the gym. I needed multiple heavy bags, speed bags, jump ropes, and much more to host classes and clients effectively. It would be SUPER expensive to purchase all of my equipment needs, and I didn't want to pay full price for each item. So, I reached out to EVERY boxing equipment supplier in the country to ask if we could negotiate a deal for me to buy boxing equipment in bulk to save myself money. All of the boxing equipment companies turned me down (but one). I negotiated a deal with that company and saved thousands of dollars to fill my gym with the necessary equipment I wanted. It was a great deal for me, and the boxing supply company received THOUSANDS of dollars in sales in return. This is a great example of the importance and benefits of negotiation because it was a "win-win." The company got more revenue from not just that one initial large purchase, but I became a lifelong customer with them from our ongoing relationship. I also saved thousands on my first deal with that company and continue to buy items from them in bulk until this day (which saves my bottom line).

Parents can help their child(ren) learn to negotiate by reducing the stigma surrounding the idea that it's a "bad thing" to speak up and ask for a better situation. It's actually healthy to ask for what you want and to figure out how to make connections to try to build a mutually beneficial relationship. Negotiations don't have to be mean and "cut-throat" in order to work out a better deal. If done with civility and respect, a sensible agreement can be reached where leverage and responsibility can be shared (rather than driven by greed and ego). Negotiation skills should be mandatory for younger generations to learn. Parents, school systems, and communities at large should encourage younger generations to take the initiative to develop bargaining skills. These skills will help them seize financial opportunities and make smart money decisions for their future in adulthood.

CONCLUSION

It has been an honor and pleasure to share my thoughts with those who have read this book. Helping parents raise their children through academic and athletic pursuits has been a part of my life's purpose. Before you (as the reader) put down this book and go about your day, I want you to remember at least two things that you learned from it. To help you with (or remind you), I want to recap six main structures that I recommend that parents get from reading this book.

Those structures are:

- Butler Parenting
- The 7 Basic Self-Mastery Focuses (aka "RAADD GF")
- The 5 Wellness Practices
- Getting your "D.I.E.T." right
- The 3 Adulting Awarenesses
- Learning how to "L.E.A.R.N."

Butler Parenting

Butler Parenting occurs when parents are uncomfortable witnessing their child being frustrated and respond by quickly attempting to take over their child's perceived discomfort.

The 7 Basic Self-Mastery Focuses

The 7 Basic Self-Mastery Focuses uses the acronym "R.A.A.D.D.G.F." (aka "Rad Girl Friend") to help a person remember a system of thought. Those acronyms stand for R-Routine / A-Action / A-Adaptation / D-Decisions / D-Discipline / G-Goals / F-Faith.

Routine – Establishing routines is great for creating habits to work towards changing behaviors.

Action – Action produces merits and ways to see (and earn) progress.

Adaption – Learning how to adapt helps make less awkward engagements, enhances experiences, and lessens stress.

Decisions – Decisions help focus a person's mind to work toward a desired result.

Discipline - Discipline helps train a person's mind to do mundane things that they don't want to do but do anyway like they would love to do them (with a good attitude).

Goals – Having goals is the inspiration that helps aim a person towards a desired result.

Faith – Faith creates a feeling of confidence (and optimism) to overcome hesitation and doubts.

These five categories include:

* Financial
* Physical
* Material
* Community
* Relationships

Financial – Financial literacy should be more central to Western cultural teachings and taught from early childhood education to college. Unfortunately, since financial literacy isn't taught in schools, people must make extra efforts to educate themselves through reading books, listening to podcasts, and researching on the Internet. It's not a common thought to consider financial literacy a wellness factor, but it's as essential as any other area of wellness from a financial standpoint. Finances influence what you can afford to eat, your healthcare access, physiological stress, and other important wellness factors.

Physical – Making physical fitness a high priority is essential for enjoying many life experiences. Investing in the upkeep of your physical well-being through exercising and eating high-nutritious foods is a way to prolong life (and be a parent for as long as possible). When people prioritize their physical abilities, it improves them psychologically, increases vitality, prevents multiple diseases, and so much more. If parents don't keep up with themselves physically well, the alternatives are they will experience many physical pains, must take medications to stabilize their bodily functions, will increase the probability of having surgeries to fix health complications, and much more. Taking a more preventative approach to self-care is more cost-efficient, improves life enjoyment, and increases personal confidence.

Material - Material things can be assets or liabilities. Understanding the value of assets (things that can be held or appreciated in value) is wise. Good assets include buying real estate, certain Swiss watches, or even some paintings (e.g., Salvator Mundi by Leonardo da Vinci, etc.). Likewise, understanding liabilities (materials that depreciate after purchase) is like buying most cars, clothes, or most shoes. Learning the differences between assets and liabilities is important, as it creates awareness and helps people develop better spending habits.

Community – Being part of a community is an important aspect of wellness because it creates a base of social support and resources in times of need. Being in a community enhances self-worth, creates a sense of belonging, and allows one to unite with others to bring about change. The earlier story about how Jillian Copeland created Main Street to help her son Nicol (and other families looking for a disability-friendly residence) is an excellent example of creating a community. The inclusiveness of Main Street has had a tremendous impact on the lives of the residents there (and the greater community). The testimonies of people who say, "They feel safe" and that "Main Street is like a refuge of joy" speak volumes. It shows how being a part of a community can be a testament to wellness, which is good for a person's mental and physical health.

Relationships - Picking the right people in your life is essential. Who you decide to marry, what kind of people you choose to hang around, and even the kinds of people you frequently interact with all matter to your wellness. People who have access to you can influence your moods, behavior, and priorities (so choose wisely).

Getting your "D.I.E.T." right: D-Dietary Behaviors / I-Information

D – Dietary Behaviors

Dietary Behaviors impact a person's physical and mental well-being. The influence of our cultural upbringing from how we were raised by our parents (and surrounding cast) has created an unconscious pattern of thought about how we look at food. The traditional ways that we have been taught to eat have made choices almost automatic regarding what we prefer for breakfast, lunch, and dinner (even on holidays and other occasions). People must decide to think long-term regarding their eating habits and choose to improve how they eat for their longevity.

I-Information Intake

The sources of news and viewing consumption people give their attention can impact them consciously and unconsciously. It is important to be mindful of how what a person watches, listens to, or is entertained by affects their psychology.

E-Entertainment Pursuits

Entertainment has a way of slipping into our subconscious and influencing the way we think and behave. Some people use entertainment to relax and enjoy spending time watching something not too "hard" to watch (e.g., sports, reality TV shows, etc.). Other times people can choose to utilize their leisure time as "downtime" (which can make a person lazier in their thinking), or "High Time" (which can increase their chances of working to become progressive). I believe that the best way people can enhance their value is by using every moment possible to become a better version of themselves. By using "High Time" to replace "downtime," a person can utilize their time wisely to work towards learning, developing ideas, and working on projects they want to pursue.

T-Thought Training

Whenever people want to improve their thoughts, they must get clear about thinking long-term about how they want to respect themselves and master their positive self-talk. Conversations in a person's mind can run rampant and lack direction. A key component for focusing a person's mind is slowing down their train of thought and being patient with themselves. Thoughts are all about training your mind toward the future version of yourself that you want to become. To become good at training a person's thoughts takes constantly wanting to become a better person daily. By parents constantly recalibrating positive self-talk in their thoughts through each day, they can become better emotionally, more confident, and become more mature examples for their child(ren).

The 3 Adulting Awarenesses are: Finances / Health / Life Skills

(1) Finances

- Bills
- Housing
- Taxes
- Investing
- What are assets and liabilities
- Credit

(2) Health

- Wellness Practices (like working out or playing sports, knowledge of food choices, "What is food?")
- Aging

(3) Life Skills

- Work Habits
- Communicating
- Networking
- Relationships
- Learning Current Events
- Sports

Learning how to "L.E.A.R.N."

Learning how to "L. E. A. R. N." is broken down into an acronym for people to remember: L—Listen / E—Emphasize/ A—Articulate/ R— Retain / N—Negotiate.

L – Listen – Listening to learn.

E – Emphasize – Become respectfully energized to get your point across.

A – Articulate – Help people visually understand where you're coming from (like an artist).

R - Retain – Retrain your brain to memorize information.

N – Negotiate – Work things out through patience and common ground.

There is much more that we can all do to become better role models and leaders for future generations. Modern-day parents have a tough job trying to lead themselves right, raise a family, and handle ALL of the responsibilities that come with that. I hope that this book has added some knowledge that can help make parent's jobs a bit easier. It really does take a village to help raise a child, and EVERY parent wants (and needs) help raising their child(ren).

As a boxing coach, I have tried to use my platform to be the best example I can be to model the change that I would like to see in the world. I hope that parents will use some form of what they learned from my boxing coach psychology to improve their parenting mindset at home. I have seen countless lives improved from what I apply in the boxing gym and have thousands of kids and parents that can testify to wonderful outcomes from how I helped raise their child(ren) as a boxing coach. Being a parent is the ultimate role model. By parents being better leaders for themselves (and their kids), their impact on the future will be far appreciated beyond what they could ever believe or ask for. When parents become the embodiment of integrity, their children become the best version of themselves. Parenting is the hardest job in the world, and when you apply what's been suggested throughout this book to improve your parenting behavior, your future impact in your children's eyes will become legendary. On behalf of the greater society, I want to sincerely thank you for taking time out of your busy schedule to become a better parent (and/or concerned citizen). We all need to support others that are wanting to do good for the greater good. I hope that you are moved to be the change that you want to see in the world. I appreciate you and "Thank YOU!"

Made in the USA
Middletown, DE
09 September 2024

60645826R00090